CHENG & TSUI

"Bringing Asia to the World"™

MW00991178

中文听说读写 · 中文聽說讀寫

INTEGRATED CHINESE

Simplified and Traditional Characters

4

Character Workbook

4th Edition

Yuehua Liu and Tao-chung Yao
Yaohua Shi, Liangyan Ge, Nyan-Ping Bi

CHENG & TSUI

"Bringing Asia to the World"™

Fourth Edition

3rd Printing, 2022

26 25 24 23 22   3 4 5 6 7

ISBN 978-1-62291-153-0 [Fourth Edition]

Printed in the United States of America

The *Integrated Chinese* series encompasses textbooks, workbooks, character workbooks, teacher's resources, audio, video, and more. Content is available in a variety of formats, including print and online via the ChengTsui Web App™. Visit chengtsui.co for more information on the other components of *Integrated Chinese*.

Publisher
JILL CHENG

Editors
XINYUE HUANG and LEI WANG

Creative Director
CHRISTIAN SABOGAL

Interior Design
KATE PAPADAKI

Cheng & Tsui Company, Inc.
25 West Street
Boston, MA 02111-1213 USA
Phone (617) 988-2400 / (800) 554-1963
Fax (617) 426-3669
chengtsui.co

Contents

Preface

This completely revised and redesigned Character Workbook accompanies the Fourth Edition of *Integrated Chinese* (IC). It has been about twenty years since the IC series came into existence in 1997. In the interim, amid all the historical changes that have taken place in China and the rest of the world, the demand for Chinese language teaching and learning materials has grown dramatically. We are greatly encouraged by the fact that IC not only has been a widely used textbook at the college level all over the United States and beyond, but has also become increasingly popular for advanced language students in high schools. Based on user feedback, we have made numerous changes to further enhance the usefulness of the Character Workbook for students of Chinese.

Stressing the importance of learning a new character by its components

Learning a new character becomes much easier if the student can identify its constituent components. The student should learn how to write the forty radicals at the beginning of the Volume 1 Character Workbook in the correct stroke order first, because these forty radicals reappear in other characters introduced later. When a new character contains a component already familiar to the student, the stroke order of that component is not introduced again. However, we show the stroke order of all new components as they appear when we introduce new characters. For example, when we introduce the character 孩 *(hái)* (child) in Lesson 2, Volume 1, we do not show the stroke order for the radical 子 *(zǐ)* (child) because 子 was already taught in the radical section. Therefore, we only display the stroke order for the other component, 亥 *(hài)* (the last of the Twelve Earthly Branches). For the same reason, when 亥 appears in the new character 刻 *(kè)* (quarter of an hour) in Lesson 3, Volume 1, its stroke order is not displayed. When the student learns a new character, he/she can easily tell if a component in the character has appeared in previous lessons. If the stroke order for that component is not displayed, it means that the component is not new. The student should try to recall where he/she has seen it before. By doing so, the student can connect new characters with old ones and build up a character bank. Though learning by association, we believe that students can memorize characters more effectively.

Main features of the new Character Workbook

a. Both simplified and traditional characters are introduced
When a character has both simplified and traditional versions, we show both to accommodate different learner needs. In this volume, to reflect the predominance of simplified characters in Chinese language instruction, we list simplified characters first.

b. Pinyin and English definition are clearly noted
We have moved the *pinyin* and the English definition above each character for easy recognition and review.

c. Radicals are highlighted
Radicals in each character are highlighted. Knowing what radical group a character belongs to is essential when looking up that character in a traditional dictionary in which the characters are arranged according to their radicals. To a certain extent, radicals can also help the student decipher the meaning of a character. For example, characters containing the radical 贝 / 貝 *(bèi)* (shell), such as 贵 / 貴 *(guì)* (expensive), and 货 / 貨 *(huò)* (merchandise), are often associated with money or value. The student can group the characters that share the same radical together and learn them by association.

d. Stroke order is prominently displayed
Another important feature is the numbering of each stroke in the order of its appearance. Each number is marked at the beginning of that particular stroke. We firmly believe that it is essential to write a character in the correct stroke order, and to know where each stroke begins and ends. To display the

stroke order more prominently, we have moved the step-by-step character writing demonstration next to the main characters.

e. "Training wheels" are provided

We also provide grids with fine shaded lines inside to help the student better envision and balance their characters when practicing. When a character is presented in both simplified and traditional versions, we encourage students to use all of the boxes to practice writing their preferred version, not just the boxes that are adjacent to their preferred version.

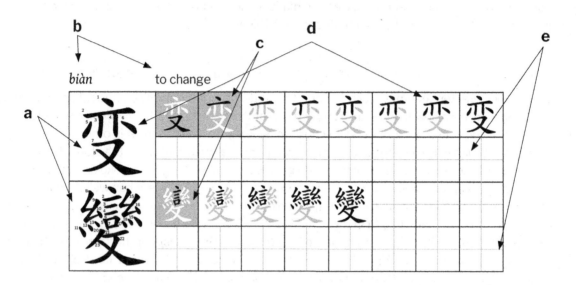

Other changes

In response to user feedback, we have updated the traditional characters to ensure they match the standard set currently used in Taiwan. For reference, we have consulted the Taiwan Ministry of Education's *Revised Chinese Dictionary*. This change has been overseen by the editors.

In order to focus on character recognition and acquisition, we have decided not to include elements having to do with phonetic identification and phrase recognition.

To help the student look up characters more easily, we have decided to limit the indices to two: one arranged alphabetically by *pinyin* and the other by lesson. Additional appendices that are not directly linked to the practice of writing characters, such as the English–Chinese glossary, are available in the Textbook.

The formation of the radicals in this book is based on the *Modern Chinese Dictionary* (现代汉语词典/現代漢語詞典) published by the Commercial Press (商务印书馆/商務印書館). A total of 201 radicals appear in that dictionary, and in some cases the same character is listed under more than one radical. For the characters in this book that fall in that category, we provide two radicals in order to facilitate students' dictionary searches. The two radicals are presented in order from top to bottom (e.g., 名: 夕, 口), left to right (e.g., 功: 工, 力), and large to small (e.g., 章: 音, 立; 麻: 麻, 广).

The changes that we have made in the new edition reflect the collective wishes of the users. We would like to take this opportunity to thank those who provided feedback on how to improve the Character Workbook. We would like to acknowledge, in particular, Professor Hu Shuangbao of Peking University who read the entire manuscript and offered invaluable comments and suggestions for revision.

Note: Prefaces to the previous editions of IC are available at chengtsui.co.

Lesson 11: China's Holidays

jiù   mother's brother, maternal uncle

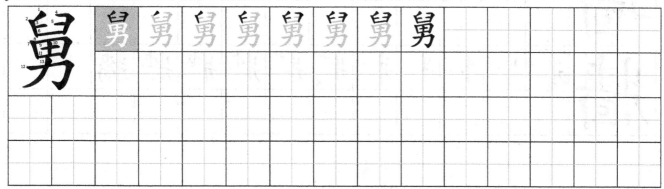

qū   district

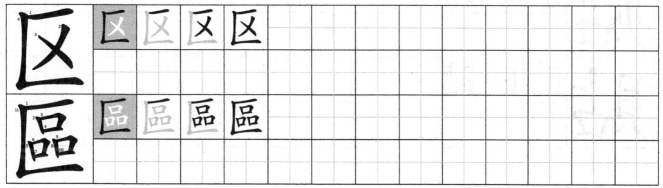

huán   ring; to surround

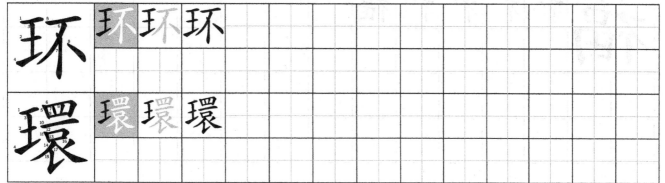

jìng   territory

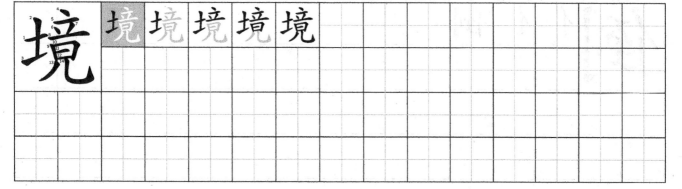

qiáng   wall

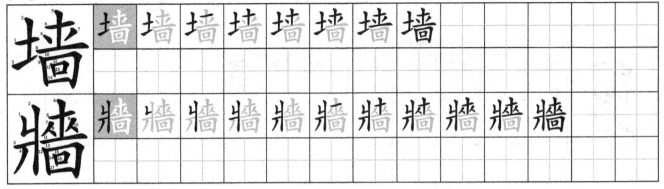

tiē   to paste, to glue

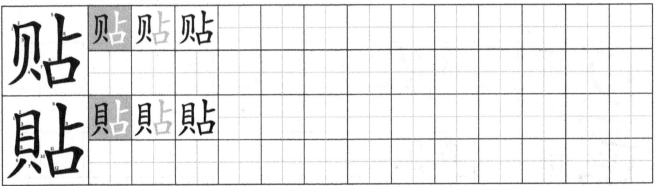

fú   blessing, good fortune

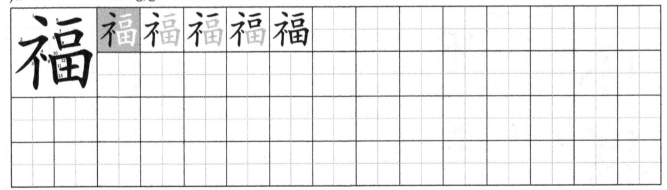

dào   to turn upside down, to go backwards

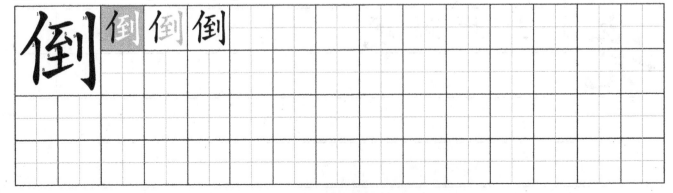

qí unusual

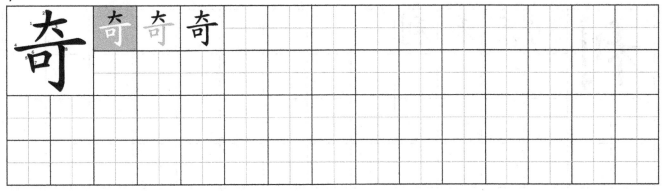

jiǔ alcohol, liquor

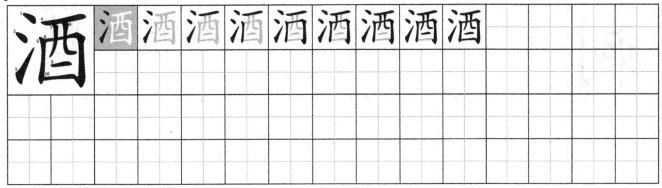

jǔ to lift, to raise

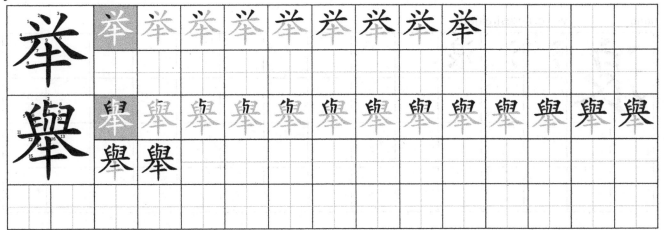

shùn smooth

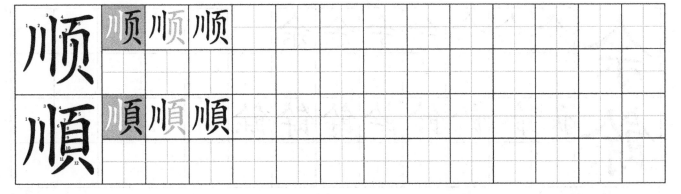

lì   sharp

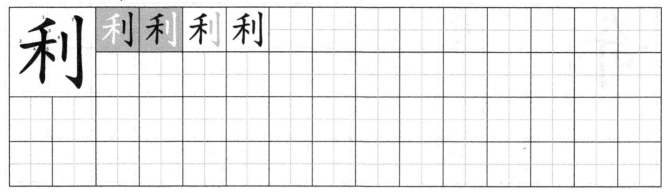

shèng   to leave a surplus, to be left (over)

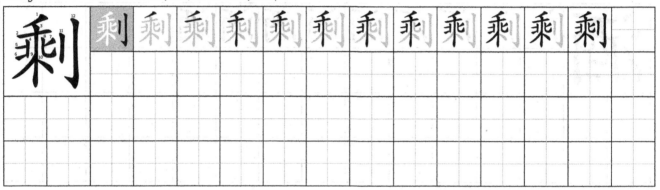

làng   wave; unrestrained

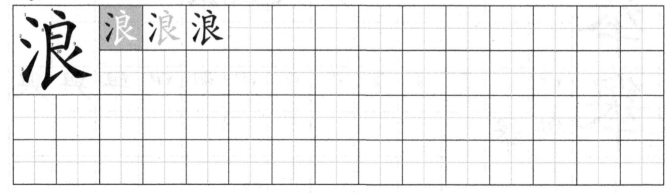

yú   to have a surplus, to leave some spare

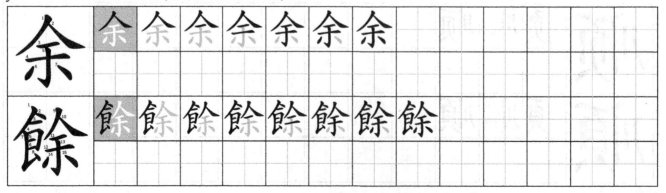

chuán to pass down, to transfer

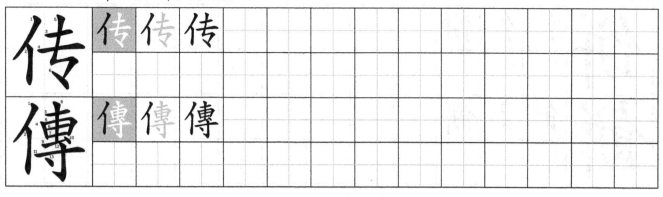

tǒng bond

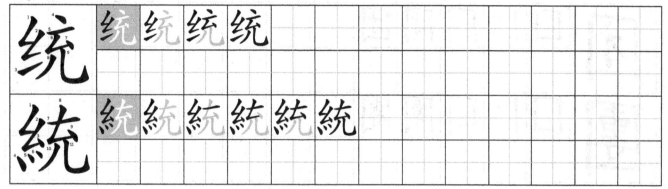

lì calendar

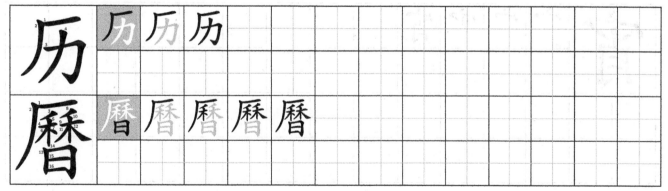

zòng sticky-rice dumpling wrapped in bamboo or reed leaves

bǐng cake, pastry

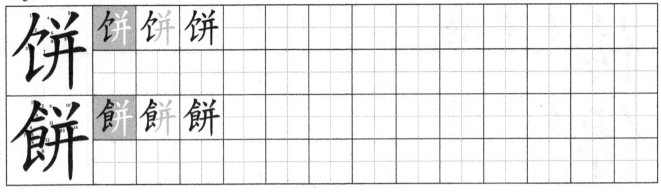

tuán sphere, lump

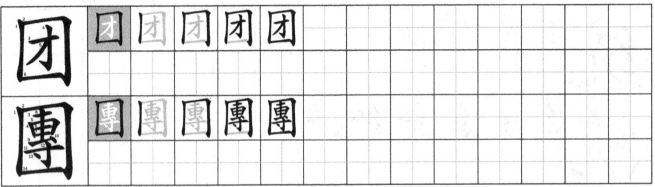

xiāo night

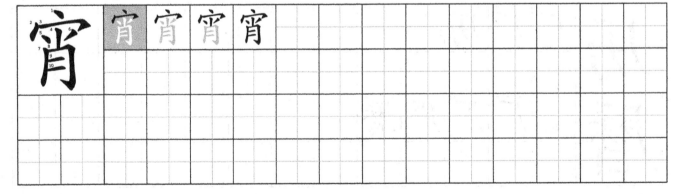

ma (particle used to emphasize the obvious)

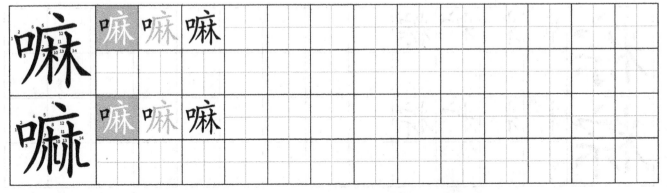

bài to do obeisance, to bow, to kowtow

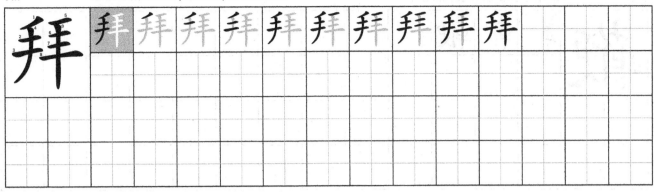

gōng respectful

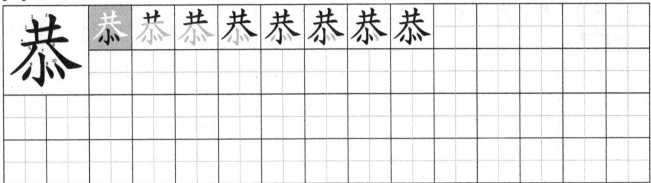

cái wealth

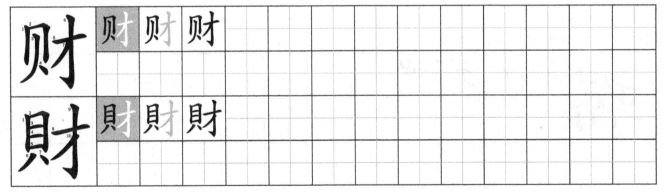

nào noisy

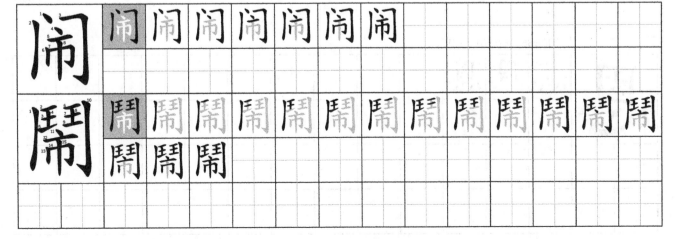

bian   whip, string of firecrackers

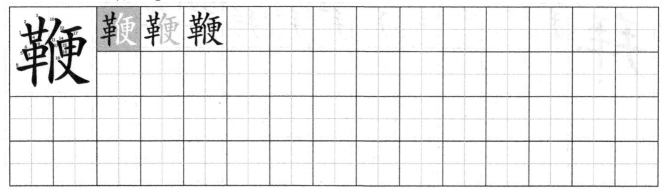

pào   cannon

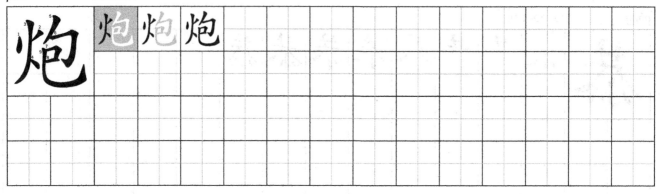

Characters from Proper Nouns

duān   extreme point, end

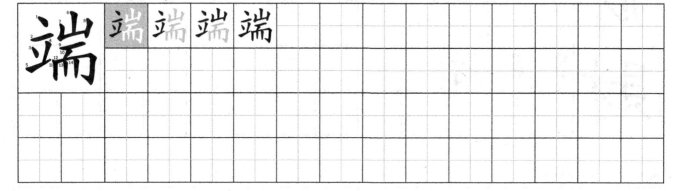

ēn   kindness, benefaction

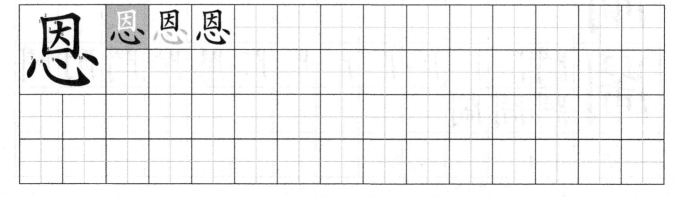

Chinese Character Crosswords

Fill out the puzzles based on the *pinyin* clues provided. The common character is positioned in the center of the cluster of rings. The arrows indicate which way you should read the words.

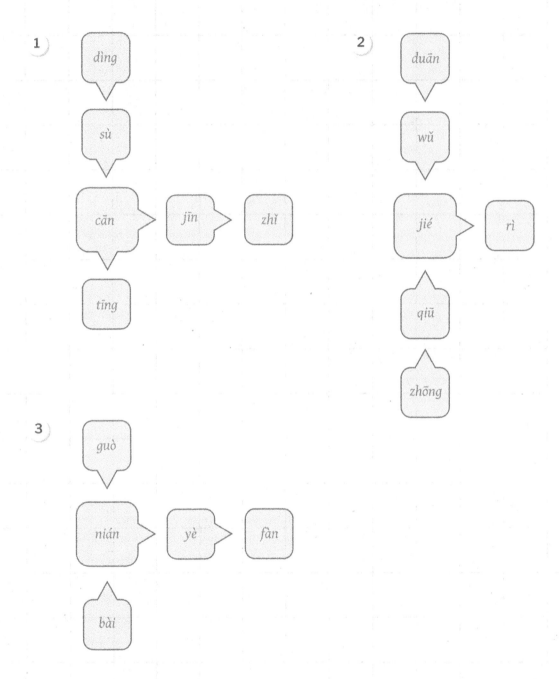

1)

dìng
↓
sù
↓
cǎn → jīn → zhǐ
↓
tīng

2)

duān
↓
wǔ
↓
jié → rì
↑
qiū
↑
zhōng

3)

guò
↓
nián → yè → fàn
↑
bài

Lesson 12: Changes in China

biàn to change

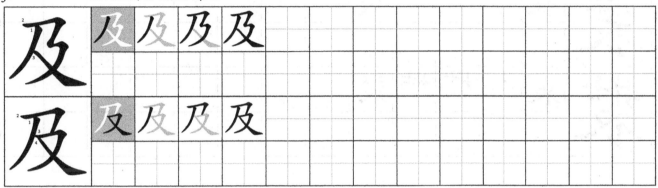

jí to reach, to come up to

jiē street

街

gài to build, to construct

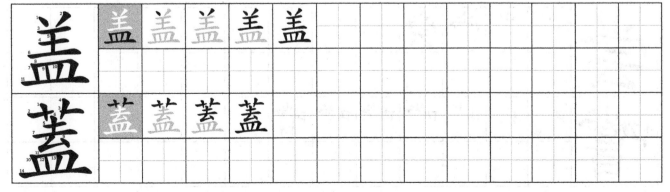

qí　　to ride

骑
騎

zhuāng　　clothing

装
裝

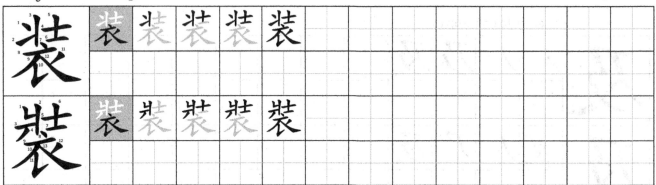

zhù　　to construct

筑
築

cháng　　to taste

尝
嚐

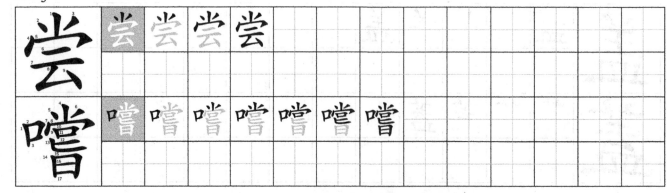

jù　　(measure word for sentences)

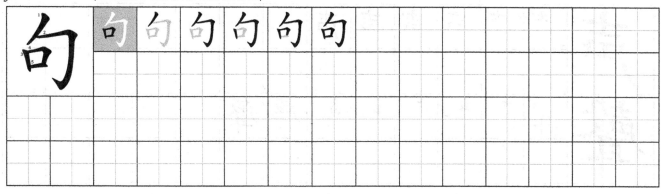

jǐn　　to exhaust

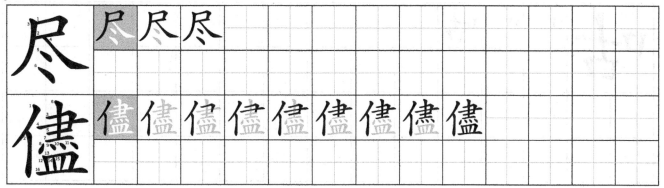

shà　　mansion, tall building

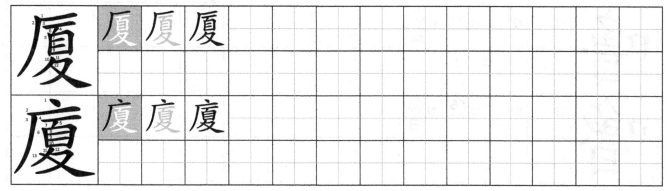

zuò　　(measure word for buildings, mountains, bridges, cities and other large, solid things)

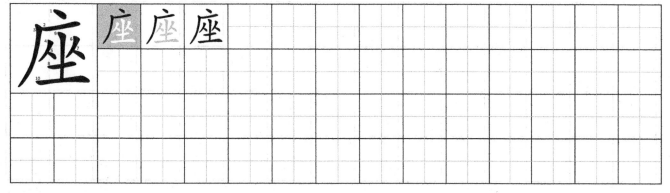

shēng   sound

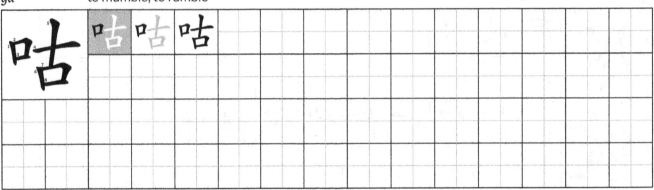

gū   to mumble, to rumble

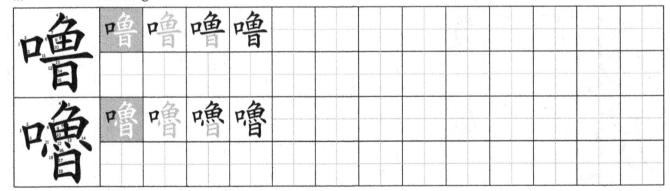

lū   rumbling

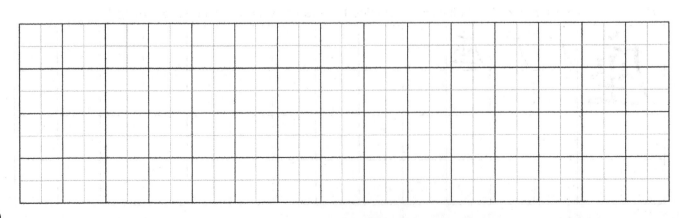

fū   man, male adult

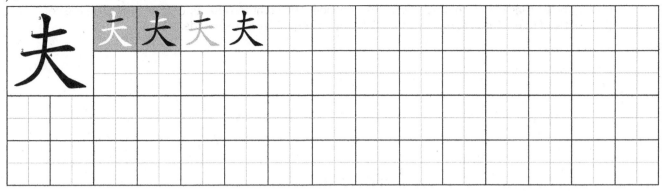

miào   temple

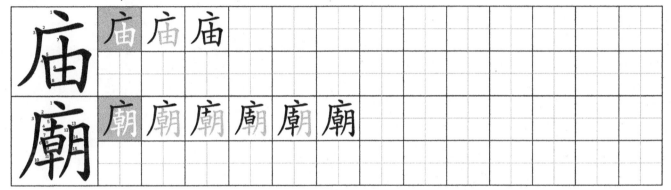

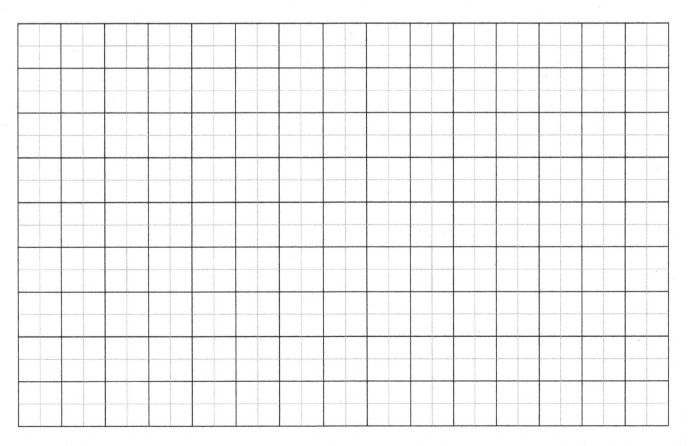

Chinese Character Crosswords

Fill out the puzzles based on the *pinyin* clues provided. The common character is positioned in the center of the cluster of rings. The arrows indicate which way you should read the words.

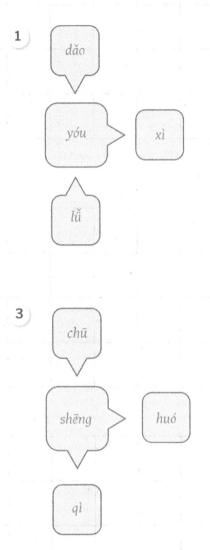

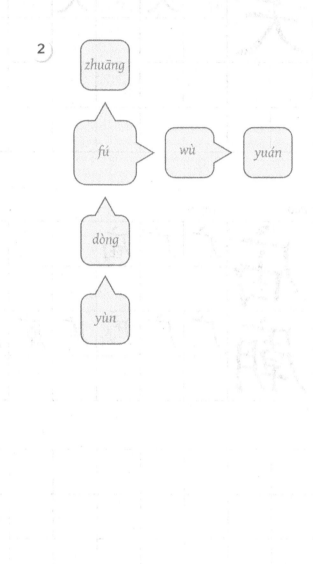

Lesson 13: A Trip to Yunnan

xiǎng   to enjoy

享　享　享　享　享

cān   to participate

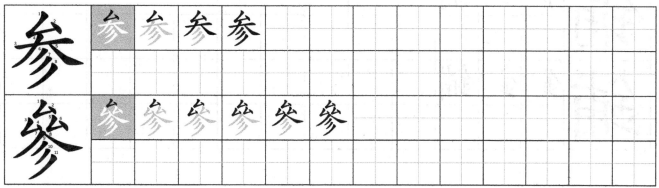

参　参　参　参　参

参　参　参　参　参　参　参

kuò   to include

括　括　括　括

tōng   to pass through

通　通　通　通　通

yìng   hard

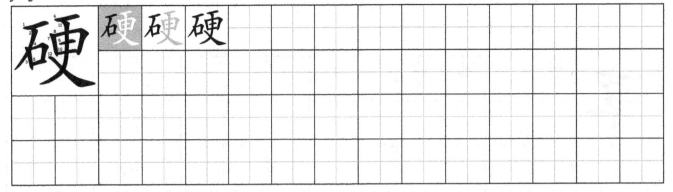

pù   bunk

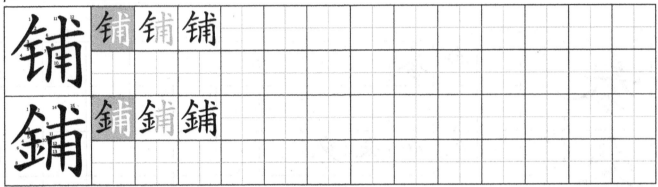

xiāng   side room, compartment

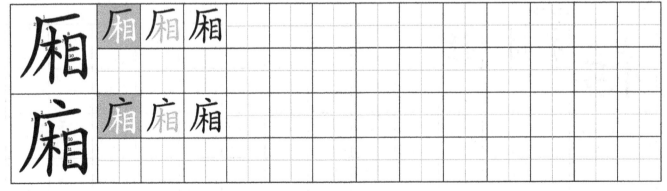

dùn   (measure word for meals)

hé   box

盒 | 盒 | 盒 | 盒

miàn   noodles

面 | 面 | 面 | 面 | 面 | 面 | 面 | 面 | 面

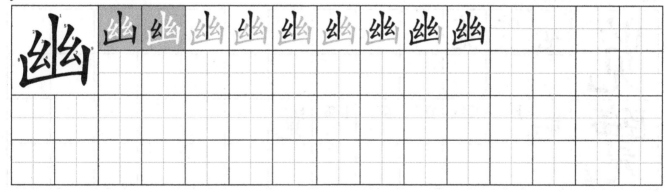

麵 麵 麵 麵 麵 麵 麵 麵 麵 麵 麵 麵 麵
麵 麵 麵 麵

yōu   dark, secluded

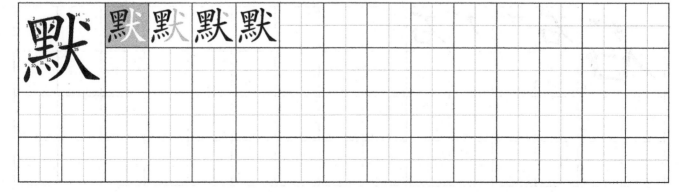

幽 幽 幽 幽 幽 幽 幽 幽 幽

mò   silent

默 | 默 | 默 | 默

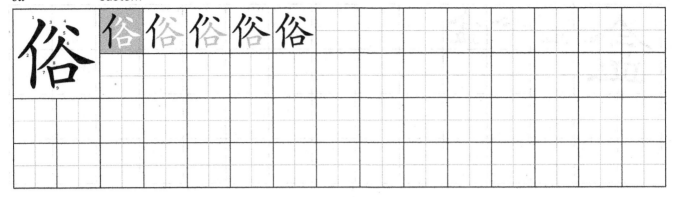

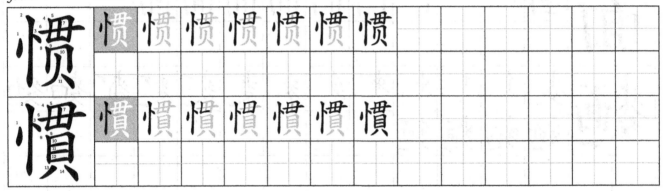

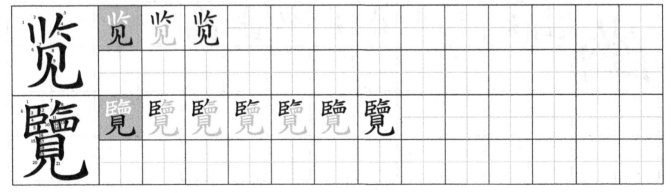

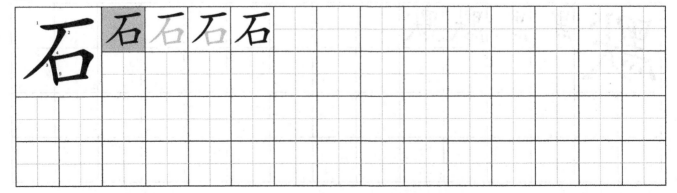

shù tree

jiǎng to speak, to tell

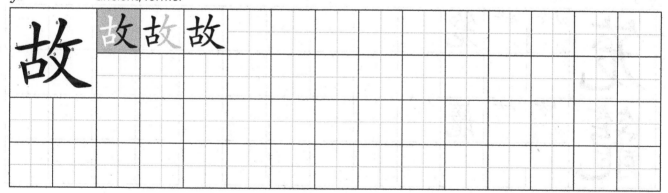

gù ancient, former

故 故 故

tǎ tower, pagoda

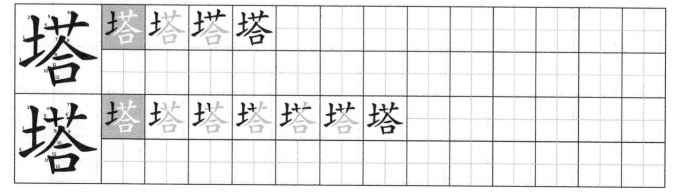

jì   record, annal

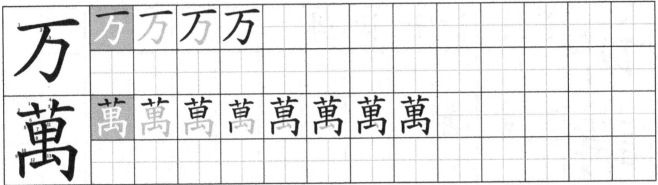

wàn   ten thousand

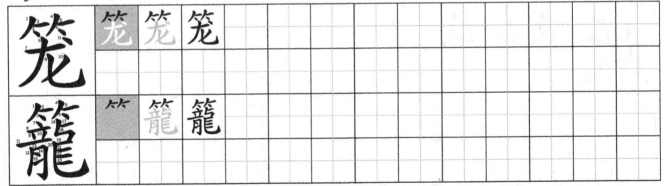

lóng   cage

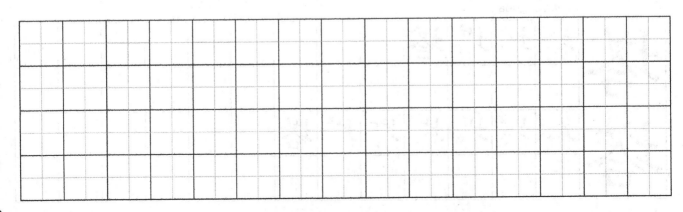

Characters from Proper Nouns

kūn   elder brother, descendant

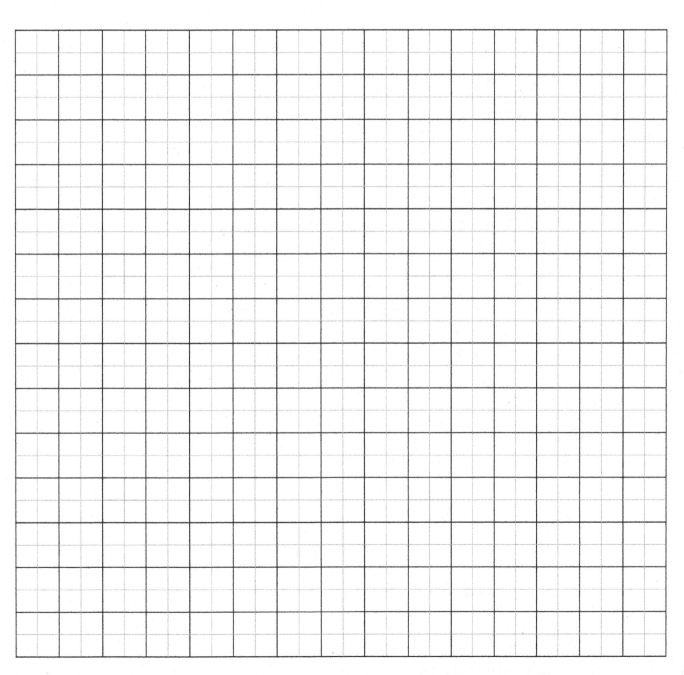

Chinese Character Crosswords

Fill out the puzzles based on the *pinyin* clues provided. The common character is positioned in the center of the cluster of rings. The arrows indicate which way you should read the words.

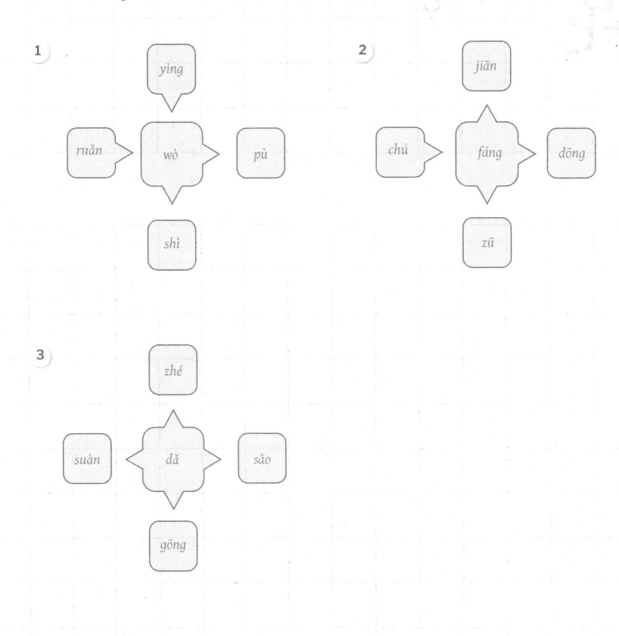

Lesson 14: Lifestyle and Health

yǔ　　　and; with

qī　　　wife

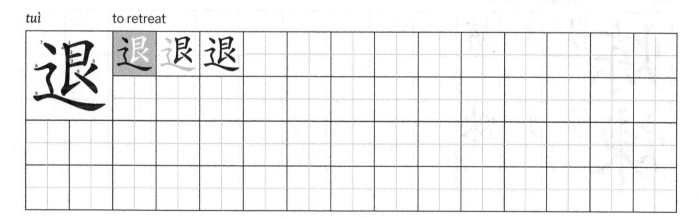

tuì　　　to retreat

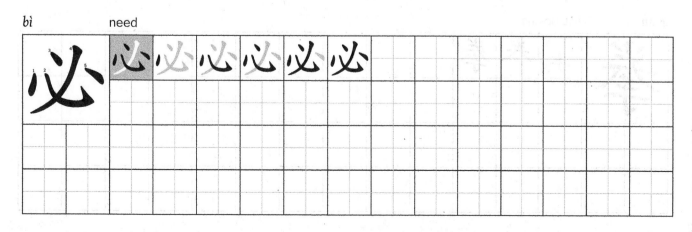

bì　　　need

sàn to scatter

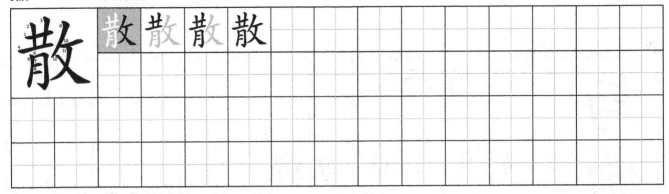

duàn to forge, to temper

liàn to smelt, to refine

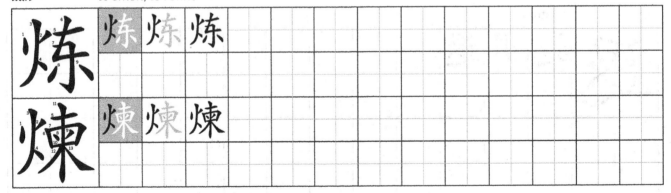

quán fist, boxing

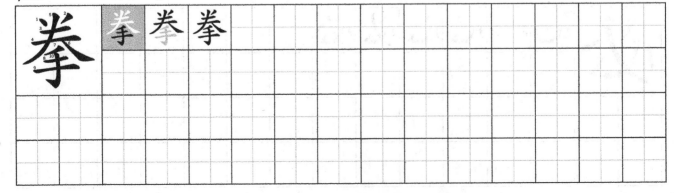

chén morning

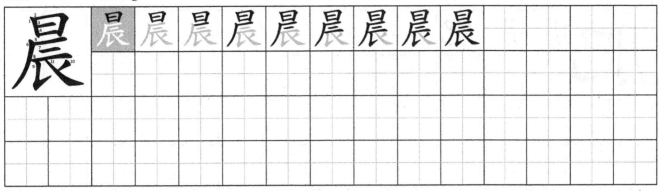

yú flawless gem

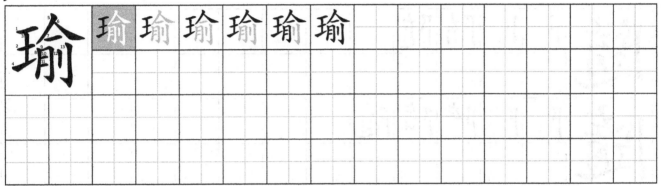

jiā Buddhist temple

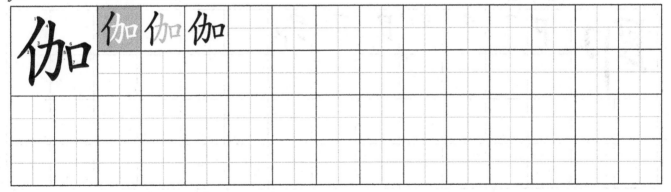

zhù to concentrate

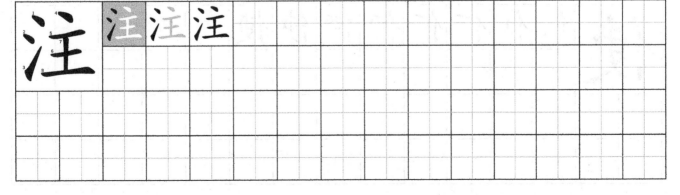

féi   fat

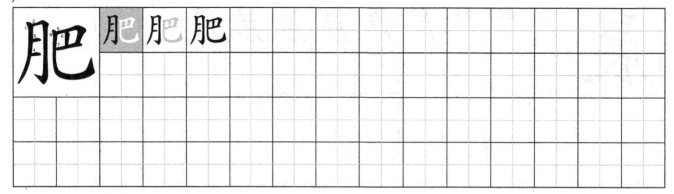

suí   to follow

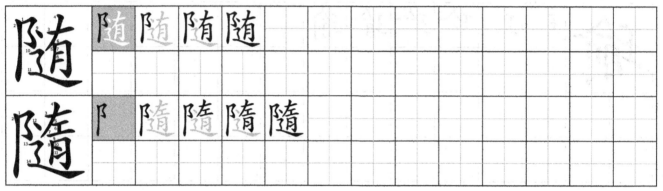

jí   already; completed

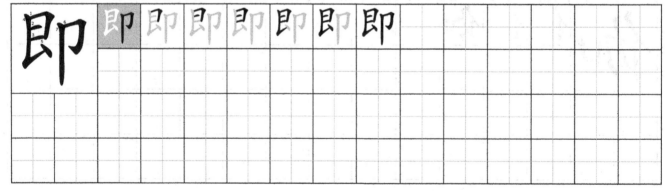

shǐ   make

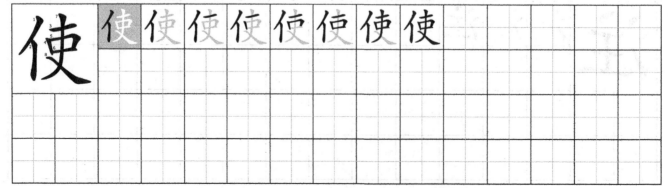

yíng   to manage

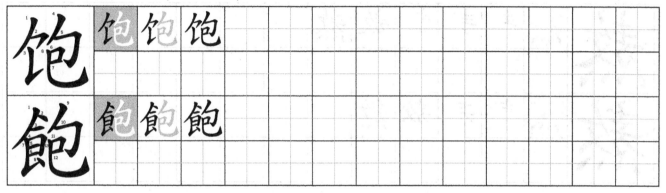

bǎo   full, satiated (after a meal)

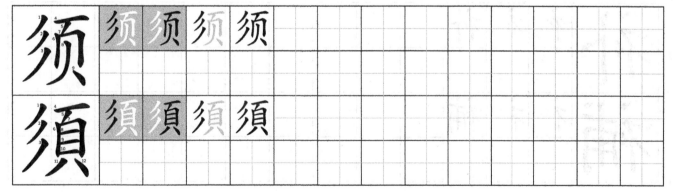

xū   must

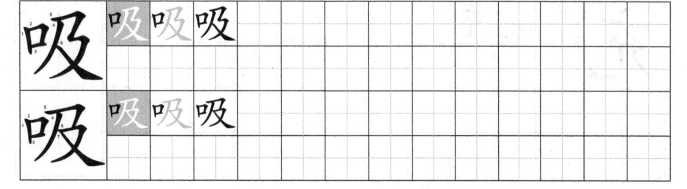

xī   to inhale

yān　　smoke, cigarette

| 烟 烟 烟 | | | | | | | | | | | |

| 艹 菸 菸 菸 菸 菸 | | | | | | | | | | | |

áo　　to boil, to stew, to endure

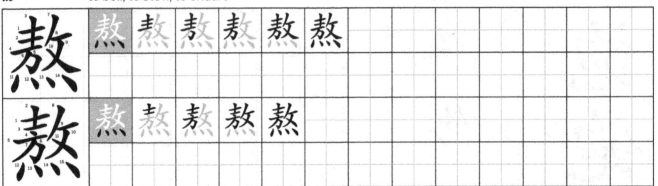

熬 熬 熬 熬 熬 熬

熬 熬 熬 熬 熬

bǔ　　to add, to supplement

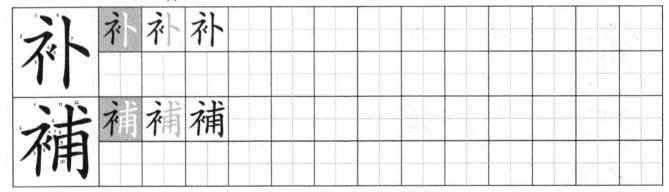

补 补 补

補 補 補

chōng　　to fill up

充 充 充

mián sleep

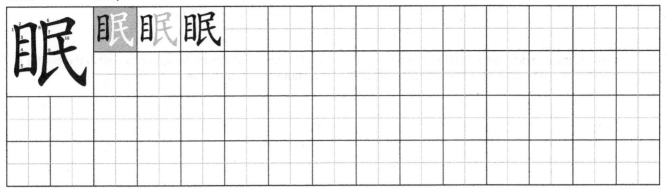

xióng bear

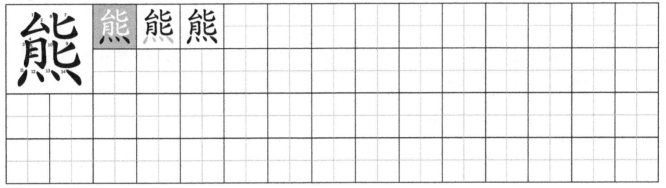

māo cat

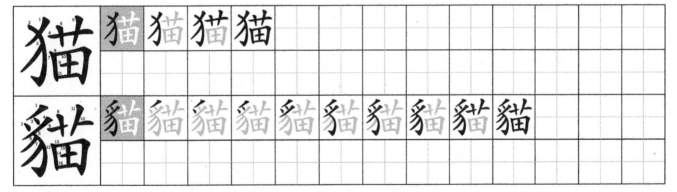

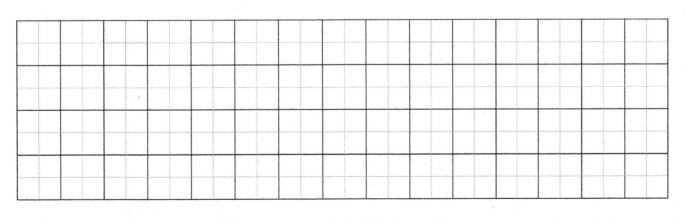

Fill out the puzzles based on the *pinyin* clues provided. The common character is positioned in the center of the cluster of rings. The arrows indicate which way you should read the words.

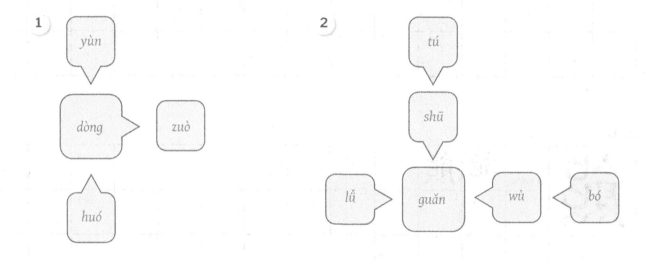

1

yùn

dòng > zuò

huó

2

tú

shū

lǚ > guǎn < wù < bó

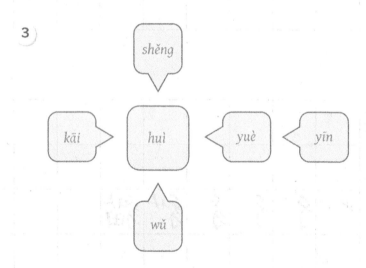

3

shěng

kāi > huì < yuè < yīn

wǔ

Lesson 15: Gender Equality

fù woman

妇 妇 妇 妇

婦 婦 婦 婦 婦 婦 婦

kuàng circumstance, condition

況 況 況 況

況 況 況 況

zhú one by one

逐 逐 逐 逐 逐 逐 逐 逐 逐

jiàn gradually

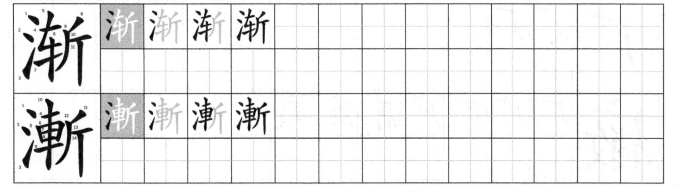

漸 漸 漸 漸

漸 漸 漸 漸

gǎi   to change, to reform

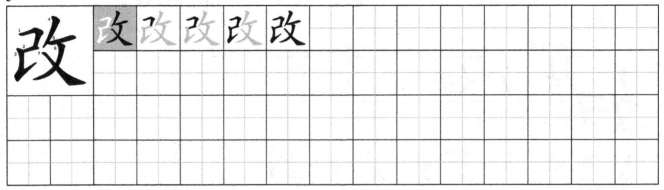

gé   to transform

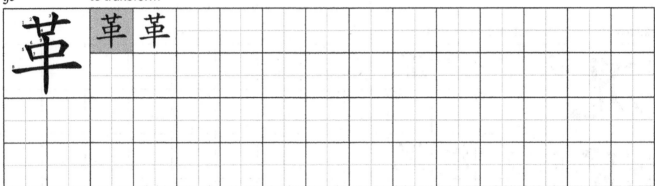

qǐ   to stand on tiptoe

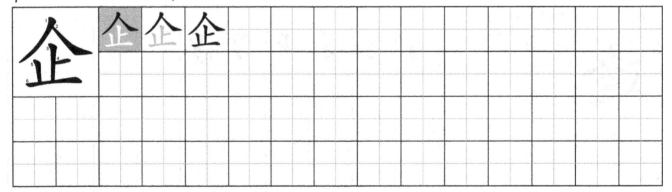

chǎng   factory

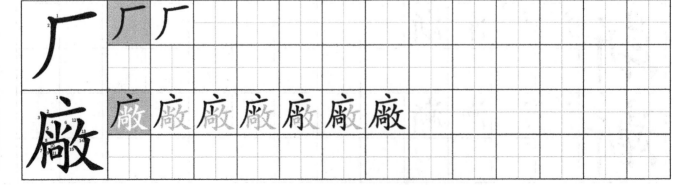

chóu   compensation

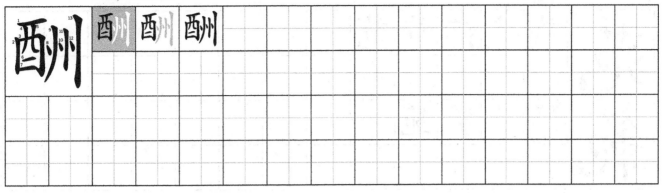

zhàng   man, husband

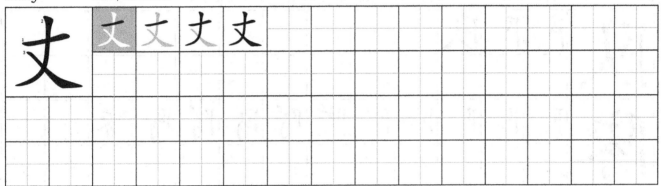

hù   mutual

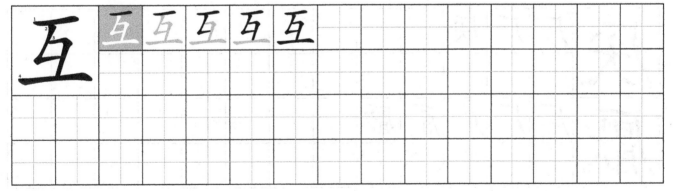

mó   mold, model

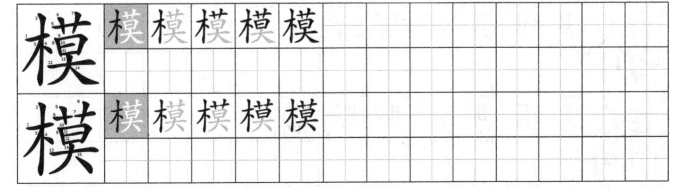

fàn example

范
範

范	范	范	范	范								
範	範	範	範									

duì team, a row or line of people, (measure word for teams and lines)

队
隊

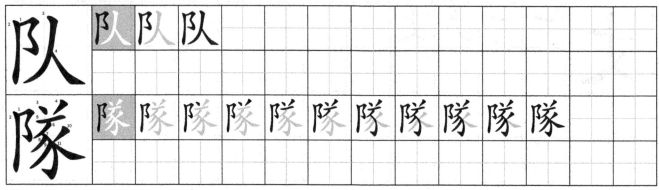

yàn to dislike

厌
厭

厌	厌	厌										
厂	厭	厭	厭	厭								

jiāo proud, arrogant

骄
驕

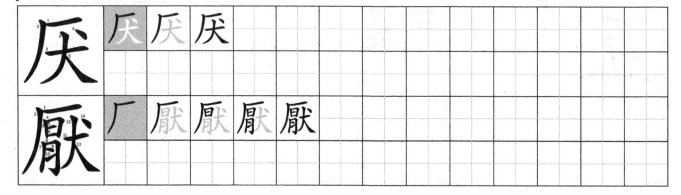

ào   proud, arrogant

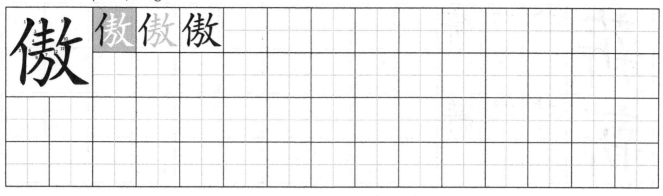

shū   to lose, to be defeated

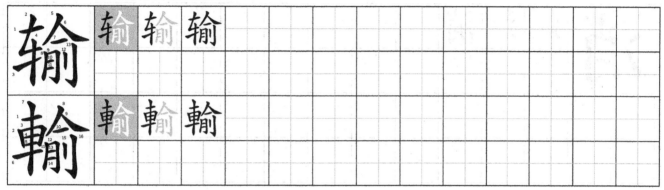

jì   achievement, merit

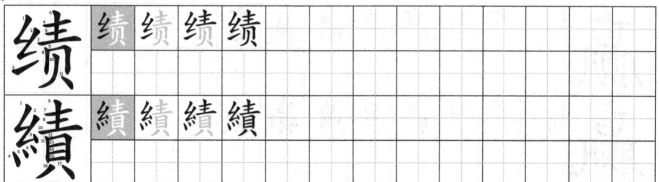

zhí   profession

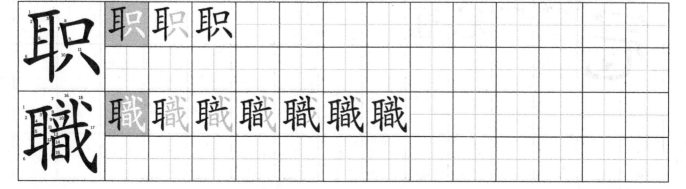

xīn   firewood, salary

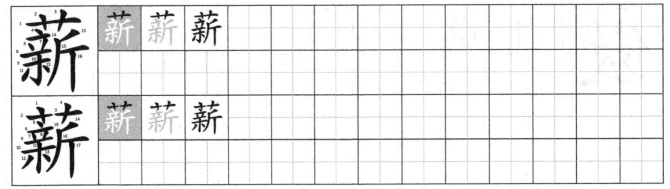

xiāo   to disappear

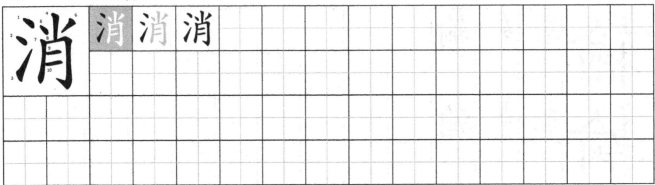

yíng   to win

guàn   first place

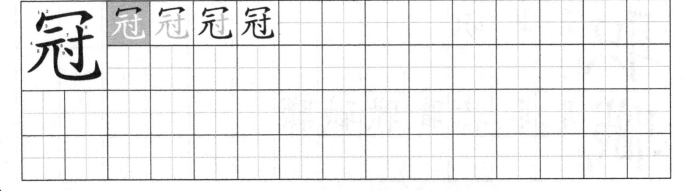

jūn army

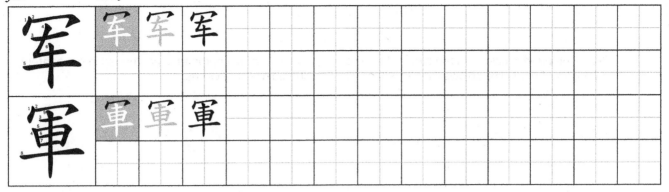

pīng sharp, high-pitched sound; ping

pāng banging sound

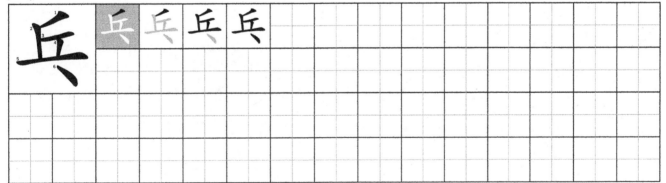

Characters from Proper Nouns

dé virtue, morality

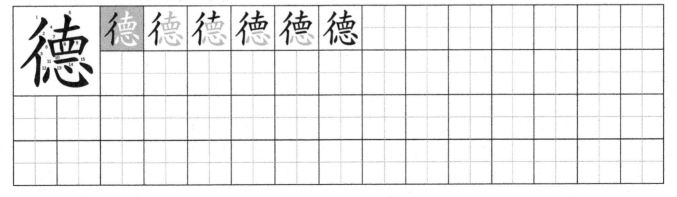

Fill out the puzzles based on the *pinyin* clues provided. The common character is positioned in the center of the cluster of rings. The arrows indicate which way you should read the words.

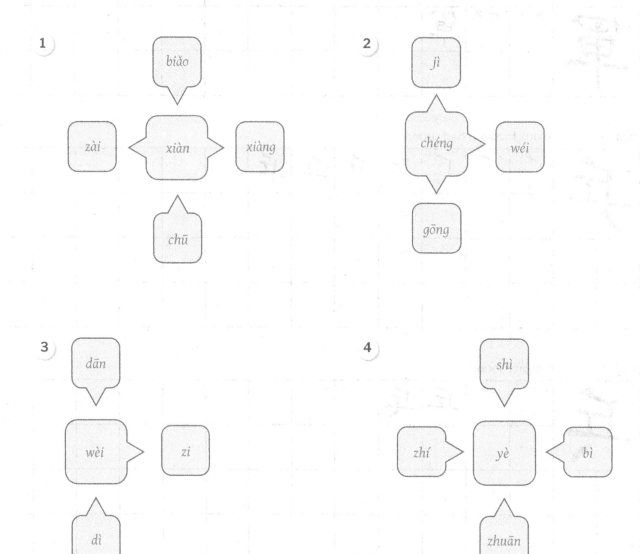

1)
biǎo
zài xiàn xiàng
chū

2)
jì
chéng wéi
gōng

3)
dān
wèi zi
dì

4)
shì
zhí yè bì
zhuān

Lesson 16: Environmental Protection and Energy Conservation

yuán source

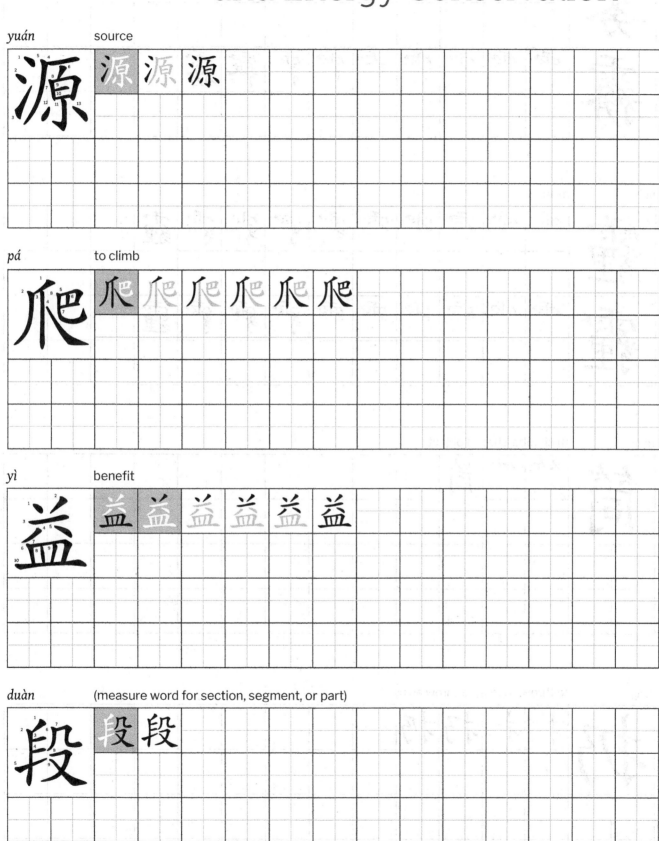

pá to climb

yì benefit

duàn (measure word for section, segment, or part)

wù　　　fog

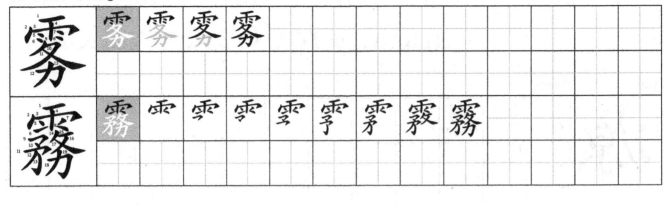

mái　　　haze

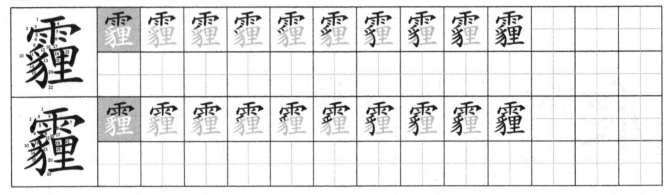

tǒng　　　thick tube-shaped object

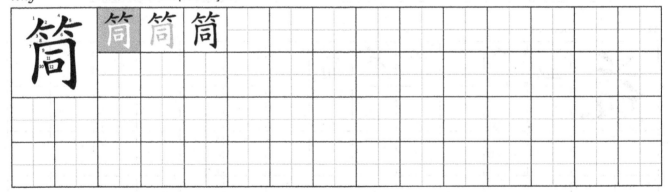

rēng　　　to throw, to toss, to throw away

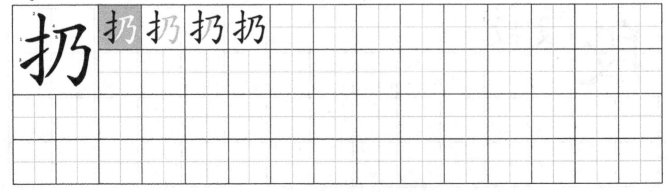

yáng   sun

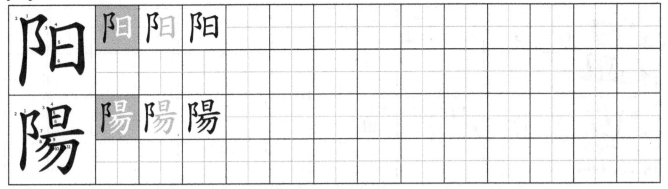

阳

陽

bǎn   board, plank, panel

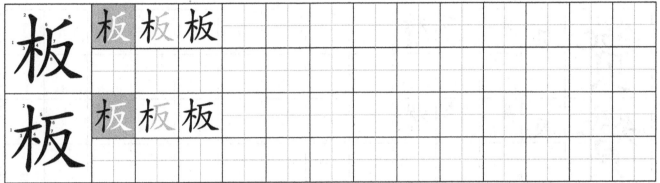

板

板

méi   coal

煤

煤 煤 煤

guī   rule

规 规 规 规

規 規 規 規

wēn warm

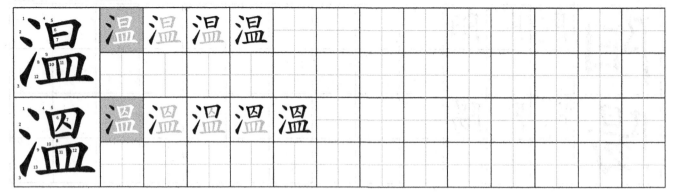

zàn to praise, to support

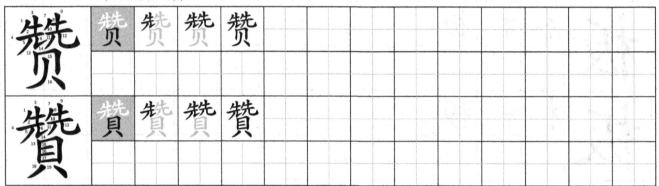

hàn sweat, perspiration

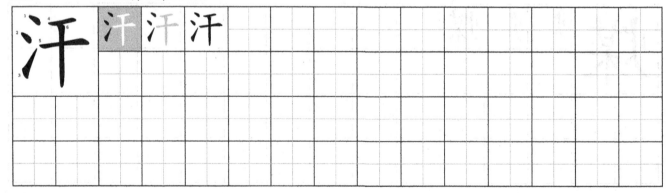

kǎn to cut, to chop

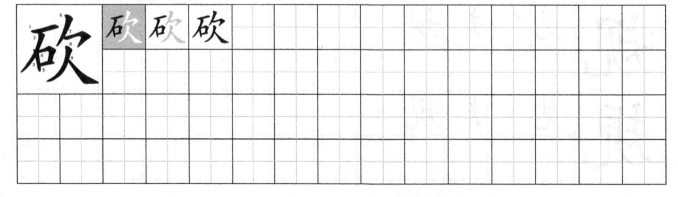

sù   to mold

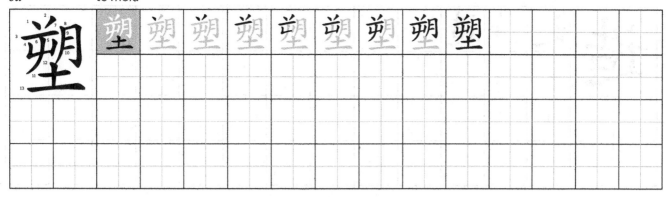

dài   pocket, bag

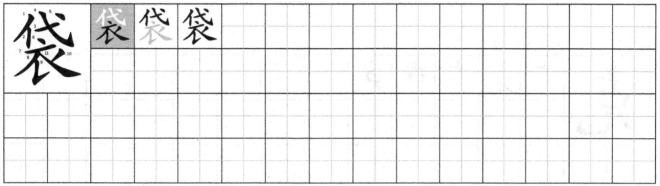

wū   dirty

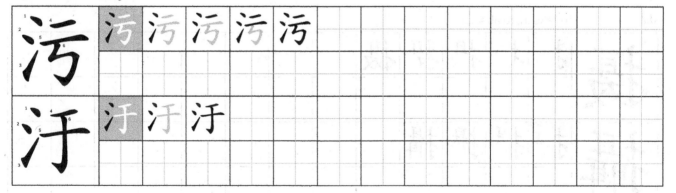

rǎn   to dye

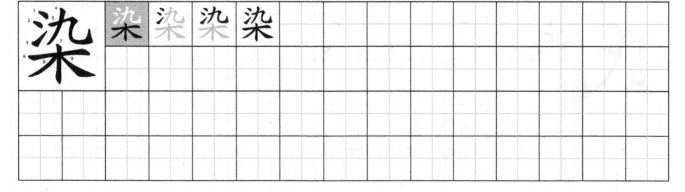

zào　to make, to cause

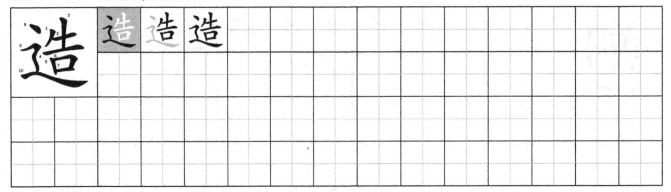

Characters from Proper Nouns

kè　to overcome

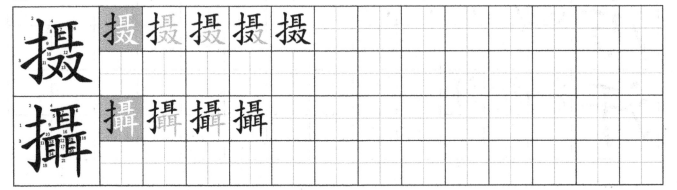

shè　to take in, to absorb

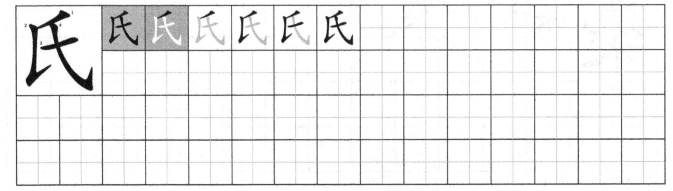

shì　clan, family

Chinese Character Crosswords

Fill out the puzzles based on the *pinyin* clues provided. The common character is positioned in the center of the cluster of rings. The arrows indicate which way you should read the words.

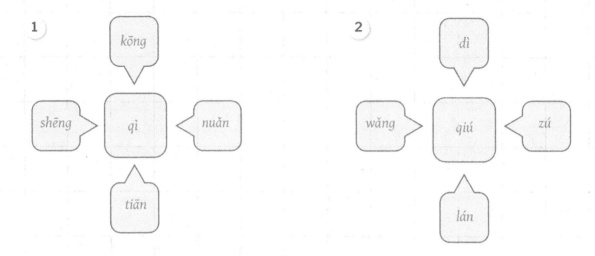

1

- kōng
- shēng
- qì
- nuǎn
- tiān

2

- dì
- wǎng
- qiú
- zú
- lán

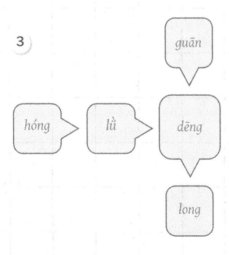

3

- guān
- hóng
- lǜ
- dēng
- long

Lesson 17: Wealth Management and Investing

jiǎn   temperate, frugal

俭 | 俭 | 俭 | 俭 | | | | | | | |

儉 | 儉 | 儉 | 儉 | | | | | | | |

tóu   to throw, to cast

投 | 投 | 投 | 投 | | | | | | | |

zhǎng   to rise, to surge, to go up(of water, prices, etc.)

涨 | 涨 | 涨 | 涨 | | | | | | | |

漲 | 漲 | 漲 | 漲 | | | | | | | |

chǎo   to stir-fry, to saute, to speculate (for profit)

炒 | 炒 | 炒 | 炒 | | | | | | | |

yǐn　　　to draw out, to attract

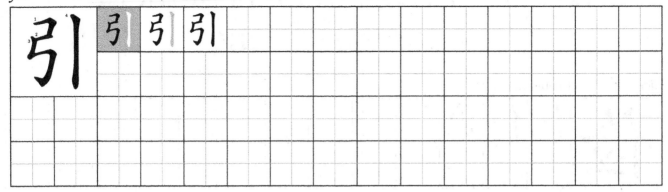

gū　　　aunt

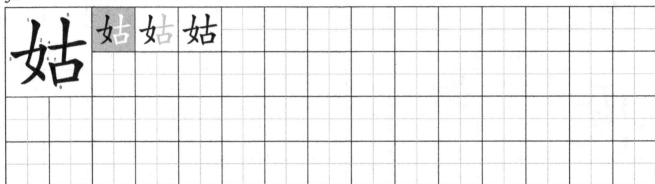

máo　　　spear

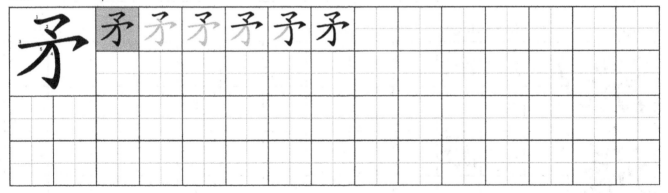

dùn　　　shield

yù　　　luxuriant, pent-up

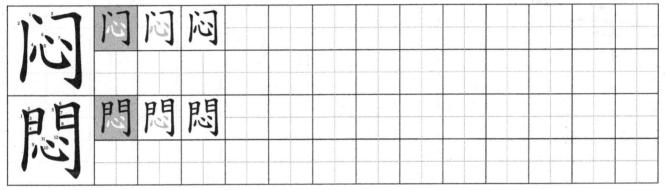

mèn　　　depressed

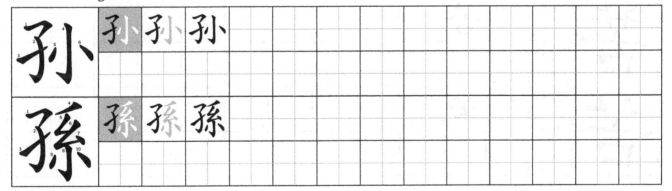

sūn　　　grandchild

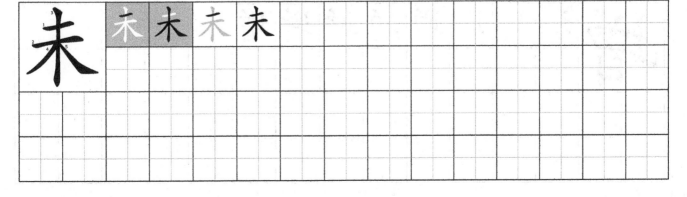

wèi　　　not yet

quàn — to persuade, to advise, to urge

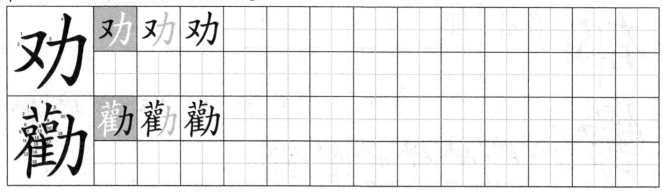

xīn — fiery, laborious

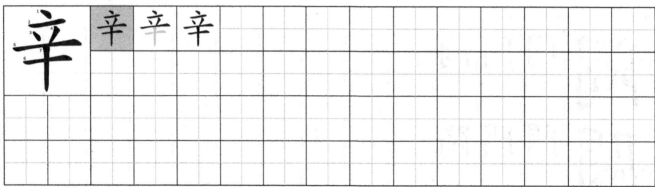

kǔ — bitter; hardship

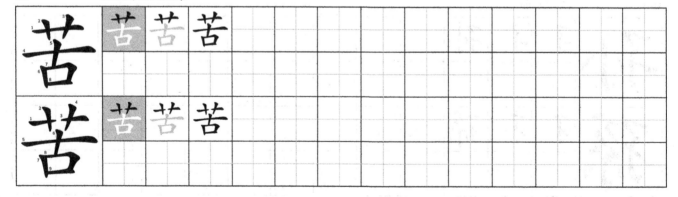

zēng — to increase

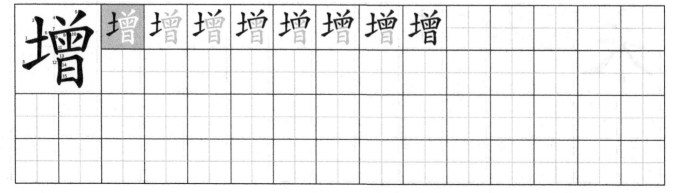

tū to break through, to protrude; sudden

突
突

突 | 突 | 突
義 | 義 | 義

yì righteousness

义
義

义 | 义 | 义 | 义
義 | 義 | 義 | 義 | 義 | 義 | 義

zhuàn to earn, to gain

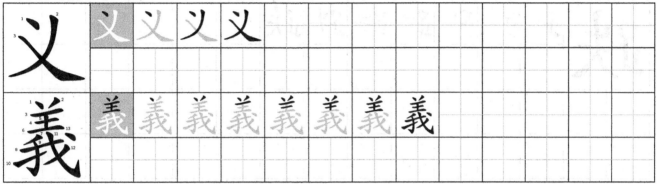

gǔ thigh, share (of stock)

股

股 | 股 | 股

dǐ to resist, to offset

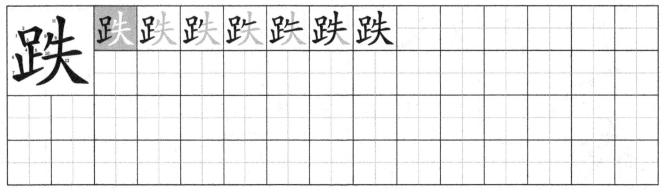

diē to fall

péi to lose (money, etc.), to suffer a loss in a deal

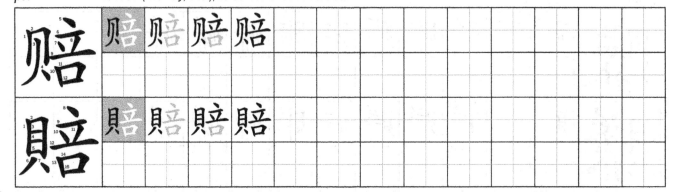

Chinese Character Crosswords

Fill out the puzzles based on the *pinyin* clues provided. The common character is positioned in the center of the cluster of rings. The arrows indicate which way you should read the words.

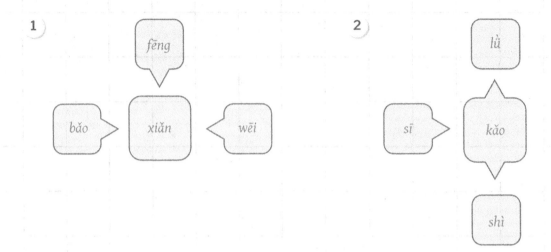

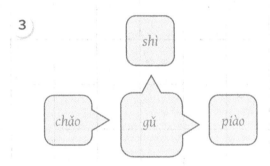

Lesson 18: China's History

zhī (literary equivalent of 的)

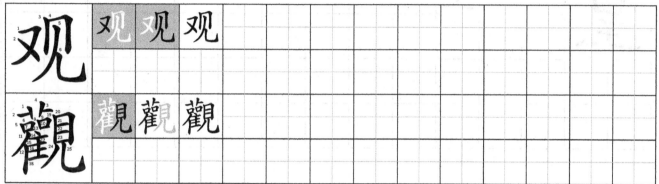

guān to view

cháo dynasty

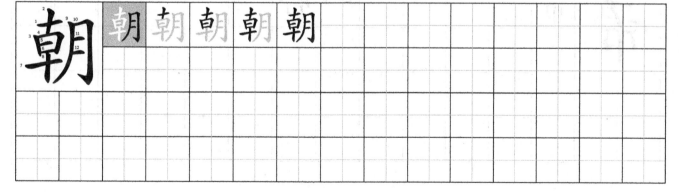

wěi big, robust

zhǎn to unfold

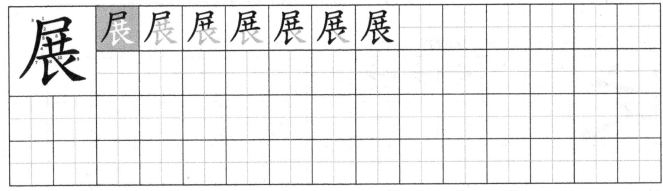

huáng emperor; imperial

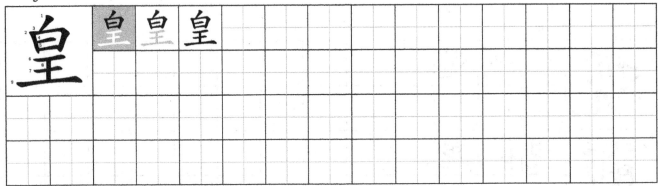

dì emperor

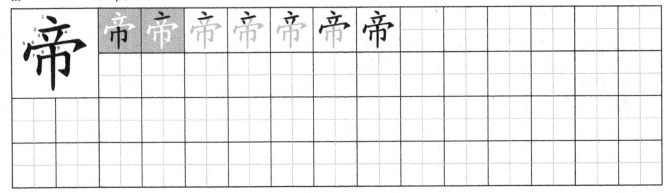

gòng to offer tribute

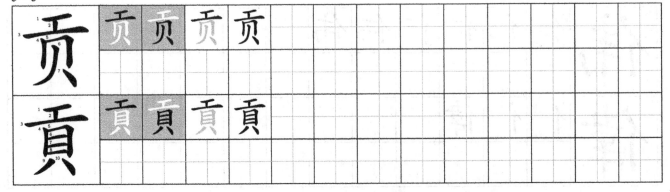

xiàn — to offer, to present

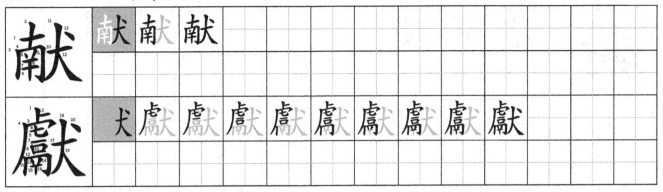

xiū — to build, to repair

shā — to kill

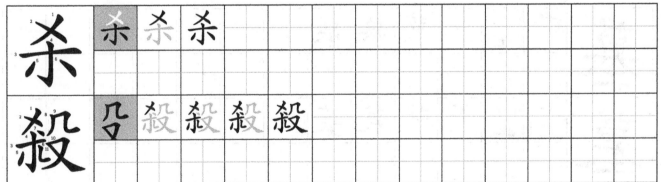

gōng — palace

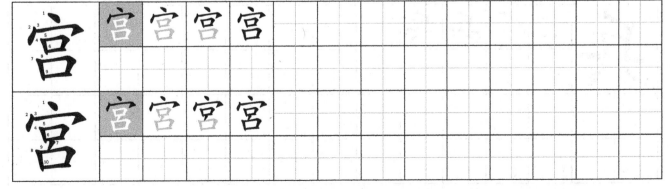

diàn hall, palace

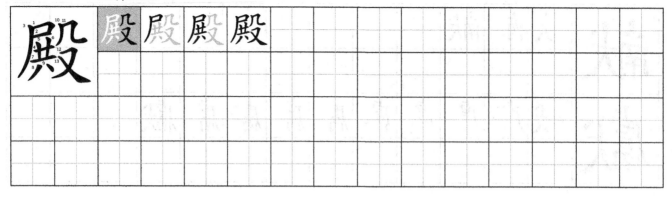

fén tomb, mound

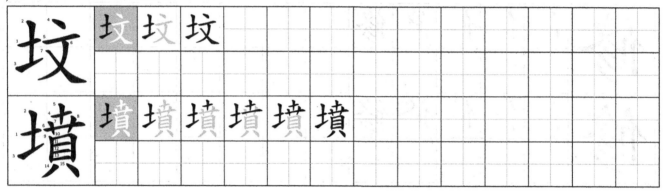

mù grave

墓

bīng soldier

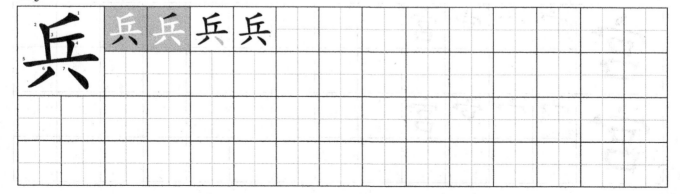

yǒng wooden figure buried with the dead

俑

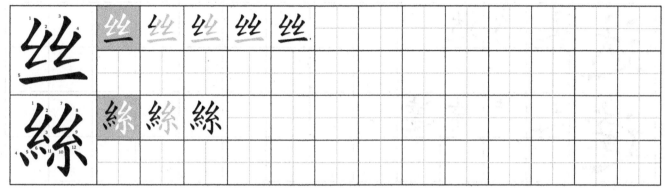

sī silk

丝

絲

chóu silk cloth

绸

綢

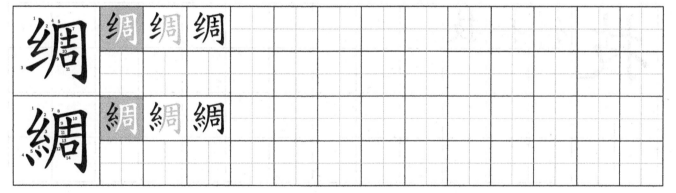

mào to trade, to barter

贸

貿

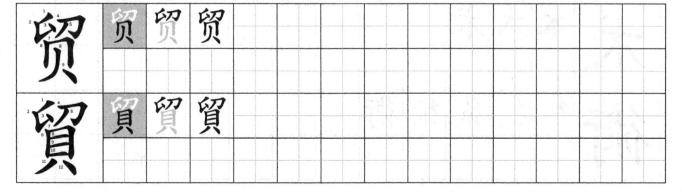

shī poetry, poem

诗 | 诗 | 诗 | 诗 | 诗
詩 | 詩 | 詩 | 詩 | 詩

dá to arrive, to reach

达 | 达 | 达 | 达
達 | 達 | 達 | 達 | 達

jì skill

技 | 技 | 技 | 技

shù technique

术 | 术 | 术 | 术
術 | 術 | 術 | 術 | 術 | 術

céng　　　once, at some time in the past

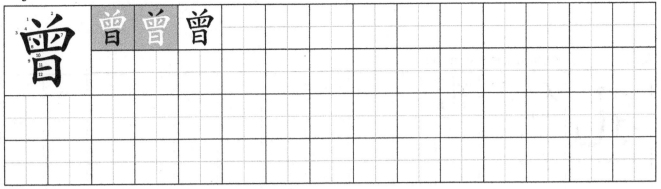

lǐng　　　to lead

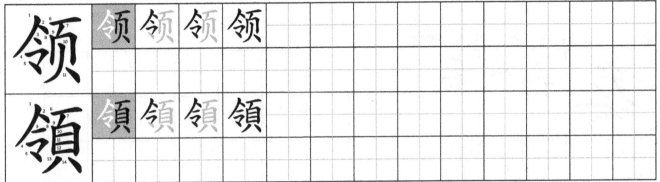

mìng　　　life, fate

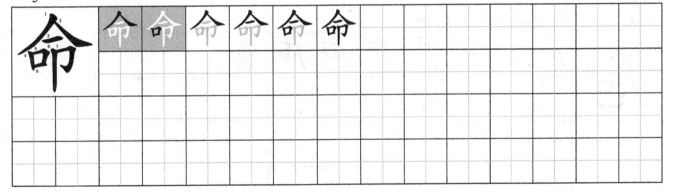

lì　　　to stand, to establish

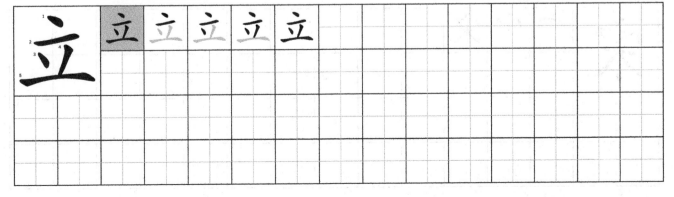

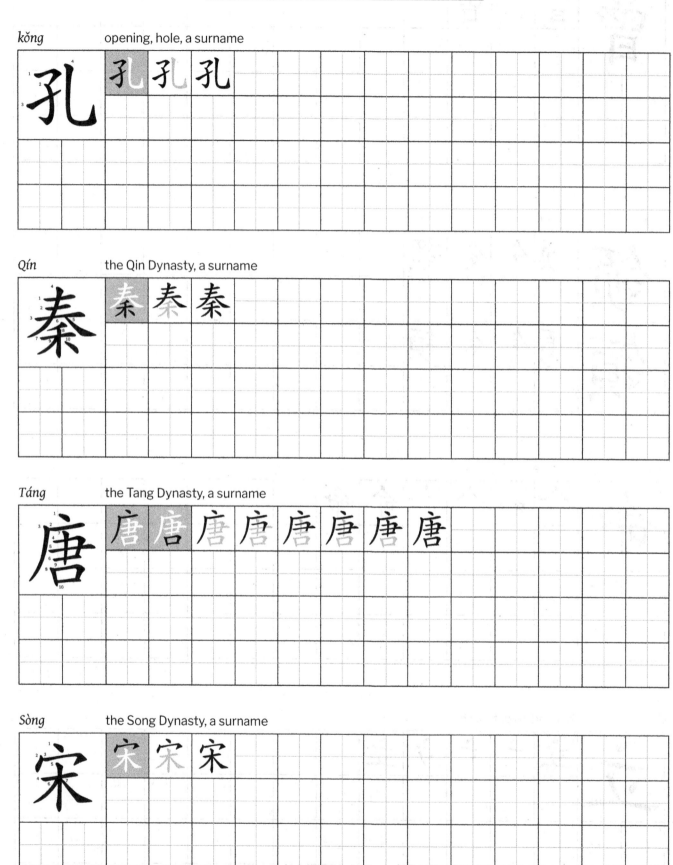

kǒng — opening, hole, a surname

孔 孔 孔 孔

Qín — the Qin Dynasty, a surname

秦 秦 秦 秦

Táng — the Tang Dynasty, a surname

唐 唐 唐 唐 唐 唐 唐 唐 唐

Sòng — the Song Dynasty, a surname

宋 宋 宋 宋

huá   flowery; Chinese, China

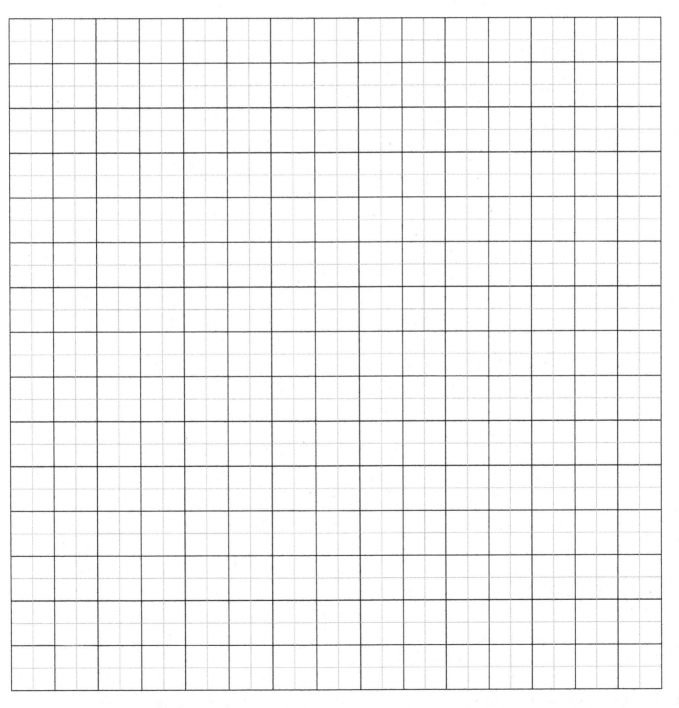

Chinese Character Crosswords

Fill out the puzzles based on the *pinyin* clues provided. The common character is positioned in the center of the cluster of rings. The arrows indicate which way you should read the words.

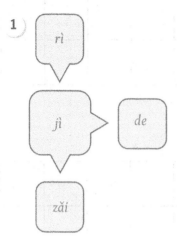

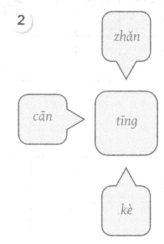

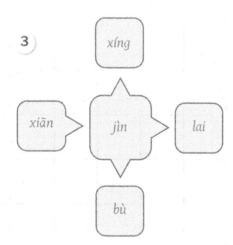

kuà — to cross, to straddle

跨 跨 跨 跨

guī — to return

归 归 归 归 归

止 ＇ 歸 歸 歸 歸 歸 歸

guī — turtle, tortoise

龟 龟 龟 龟 龟

龜 龜 丿 丿 勹 台 台 台 龟 龟 龟 龜

龜 龜 龜 龜

mǎn — full; completely

满 满 满 满

滿 滿 滿 滿 滿 滿 滿 滿

xiāo   to sell

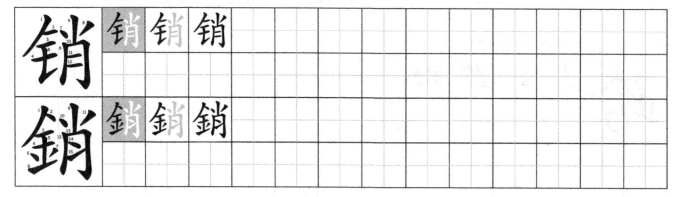

shī   wet

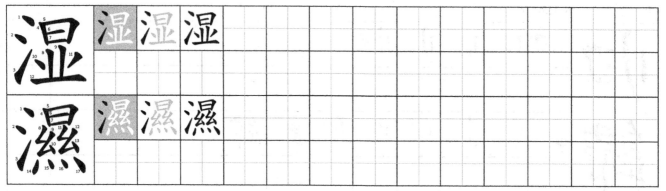

sù   reverent, solemn

xià   to scare

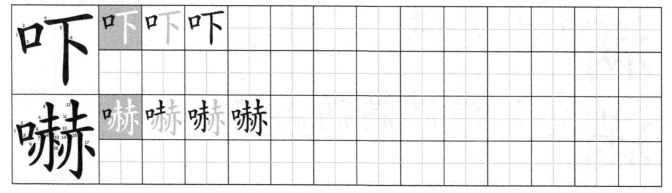

shì — to explain

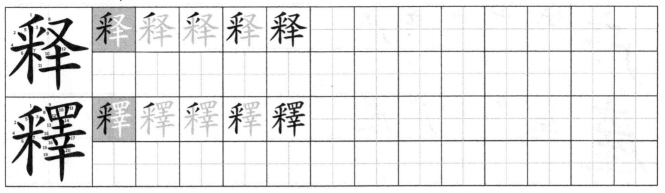

yīn — overcast, hidden from the sun

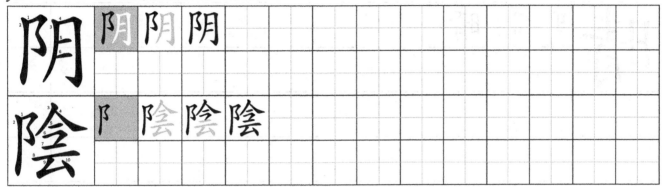

jì — to mail

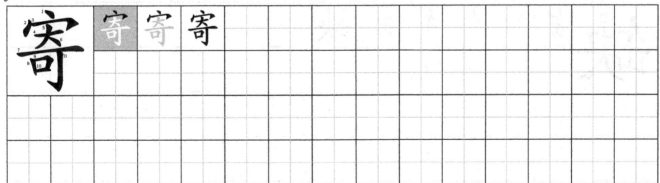

jì — already

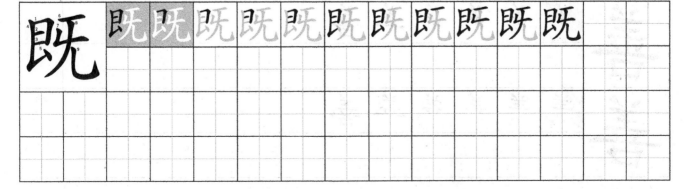

chǎn to give birth, to produce

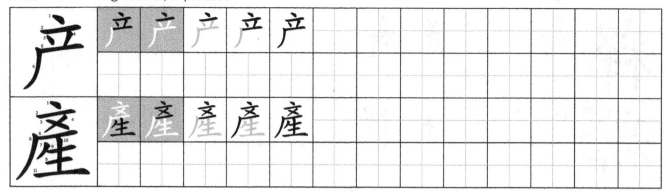

qíng sunny

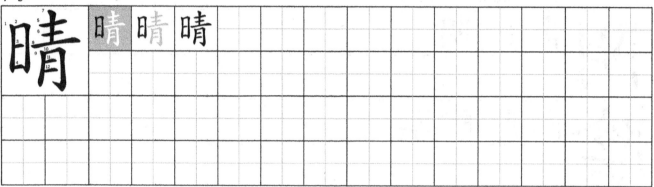

quē to lack

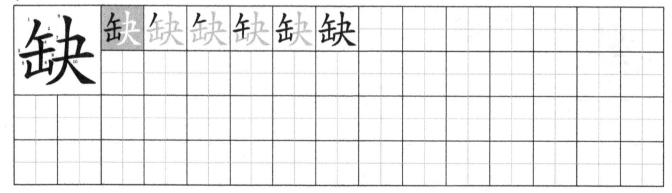

shàn good, kind

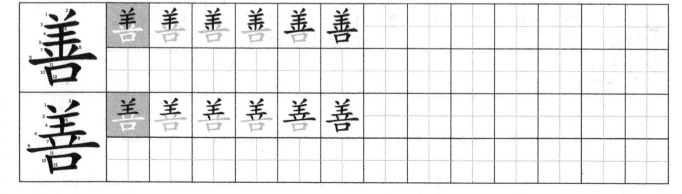

yōu   outstanding, excellent

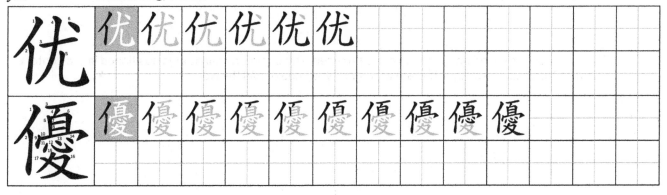

wò   to hold, to grasp

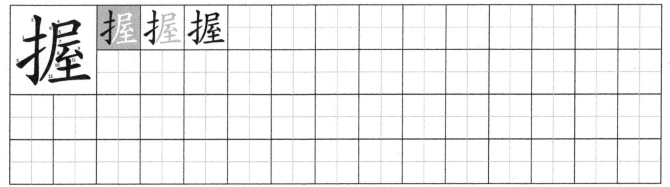

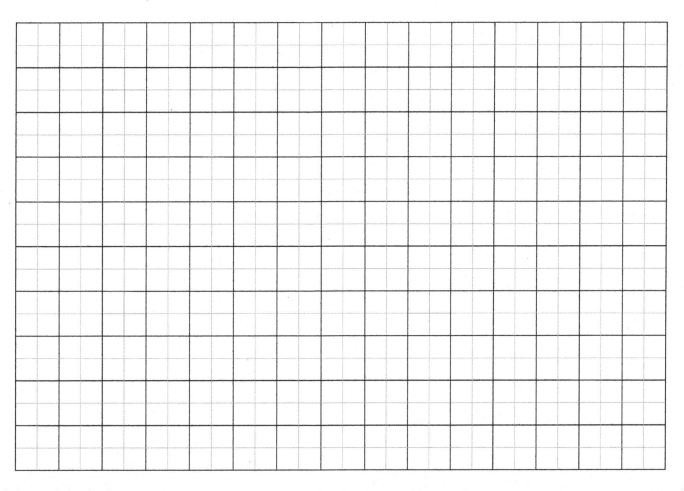

Chinese Character Crosswords

Fill out the puzzles based on the *pinyin* clues provided. The common character is positioned in the center of the cluster of rings. The arrows indicate which way you should read the words.

1
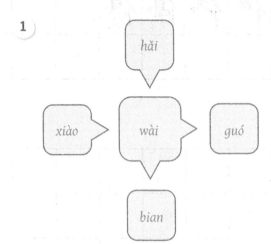

2
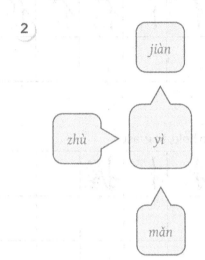

3
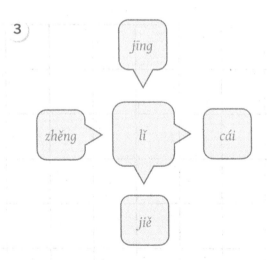

4
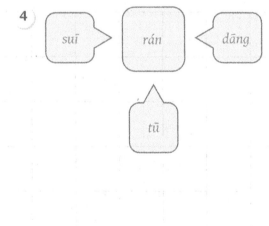

Lesson 20: The World Is Getting Smaller

jù　　to gather together

聚　聚　聚　聚　聚　聚　聚　聚　聚

聚　聚　聚　聚　聚　聚　聚　聚　聚

qìng　　to celebrate

庆　庆　庆

慶　慶　慶　慶　慶　慶　慶　慶　慶

jiàn　　to give a farewell party; preserved food

饯　饯　饯

餞　餞　餞

guō　　wok, pot

锅　锅　锅　锅

鍋　鍋　鍋

chí   pool, pound

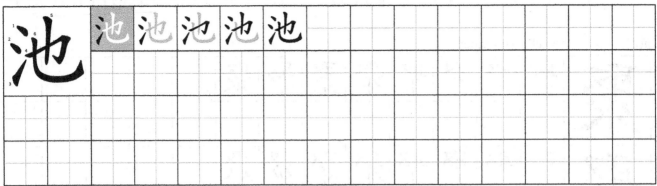

jù   drama

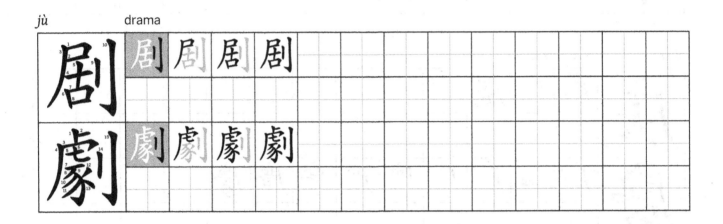

gǎo   to do, to carry on, to be engaged in

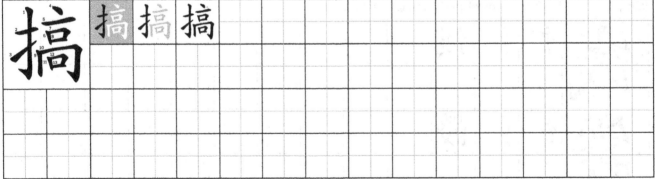

wěn   stable

yǒng　　　always, forever

永

永 永 永 永 永 永

lián　　　to link, to connect

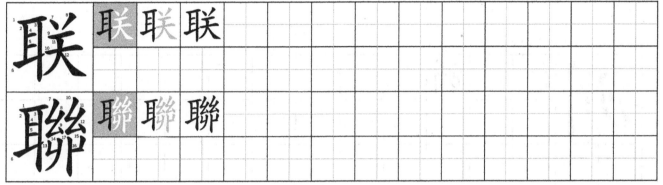

联
聯

联 联 联

聯 聯 聯

xì　　　to fasten

系
繋

系 系 系 系 系 系

繋 繋 繋 繋 繋 繋 繋

yì　　　friendship

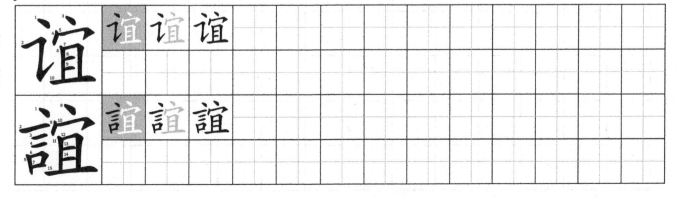

谊
誼

谊 谊 谊

誼 誼 誼

Ōu a surname

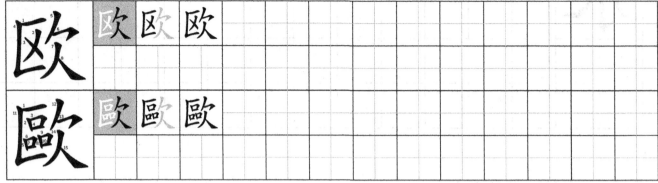

zhōu continent

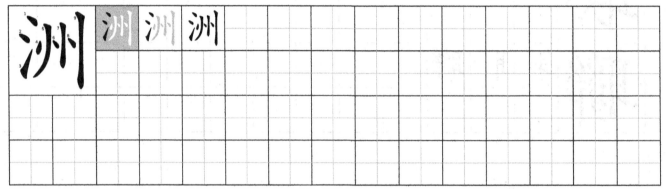

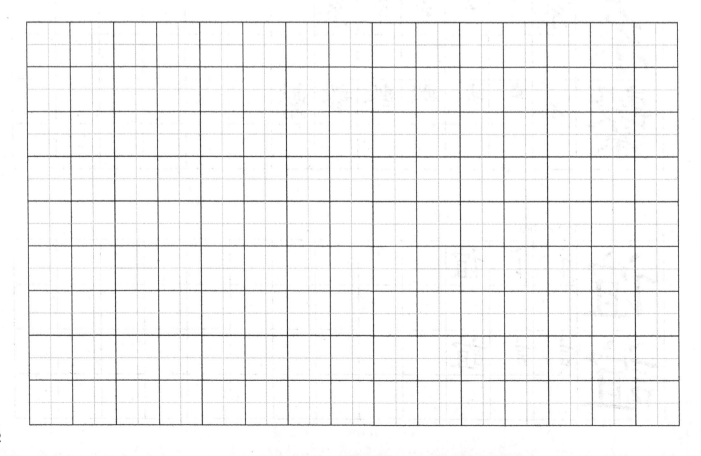

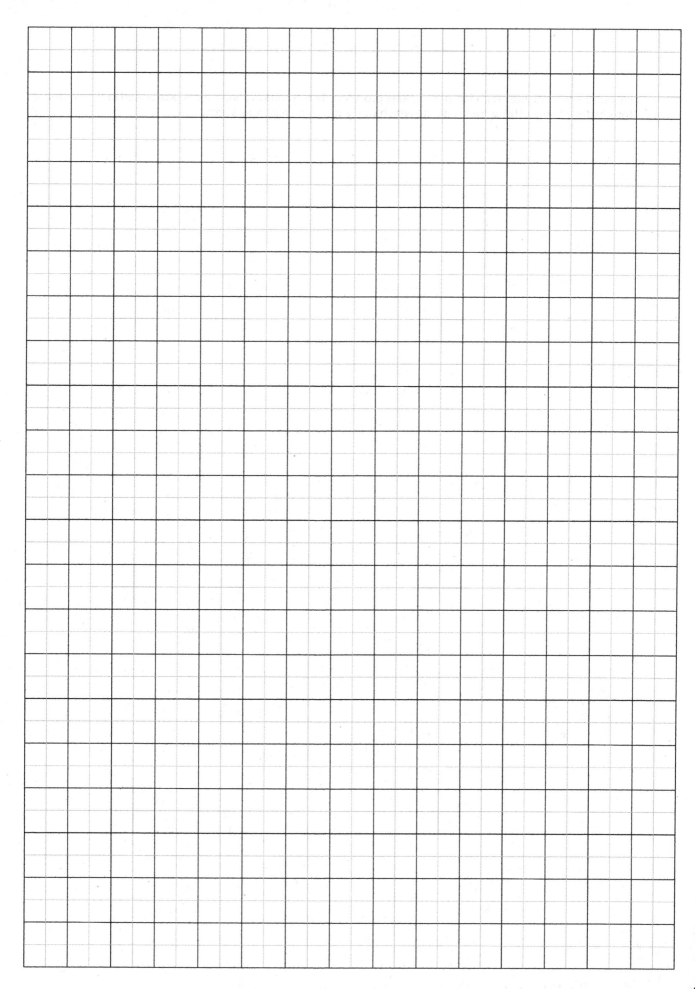

Chinese Character Crosswords

Fill out the puzzles based on the *pinyin* clues provided. The common character is positioned in the center of the cluster of rings. The arrows indicate which way you should read the words.

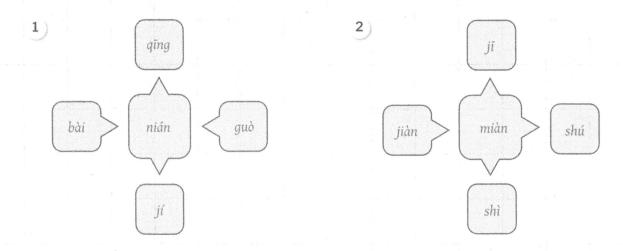

1)
- qīng
- bài
- nián
- guò
- jí

2)
- jǐ
- jiàn
- miàn
- shú
- shì

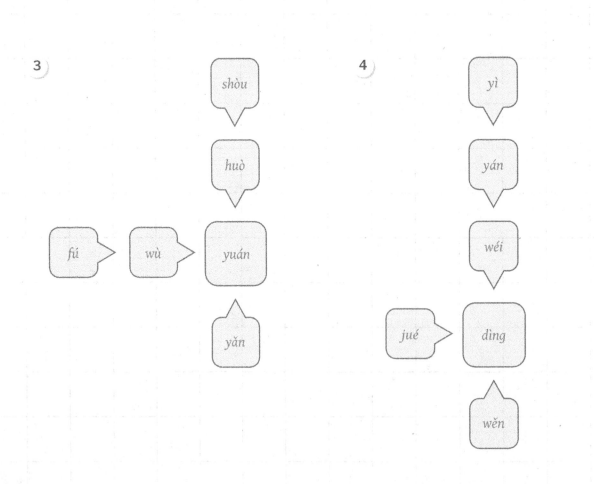

3)
- shòu
- huò
- fú
- wù
- yuán
- yǎn

4)
- yì
- yán
- wéi
- jué
- dìng
- wèn

INDEX A

P	S	T	Definition	L	Page
gòng	贡	貢	to offer tribute	18	64
gū	咕		to mumble, to rumble	12	20
gū	姑		aunt	17	56
gǔ	股		thigh, share (of stock)	17	59
gù	故		ancient, former	13	27
guān	观	觀	to view	18	63
guàn	惯	慣	habit	13	26
guàn	冠		first place	15	44
guī	规	規	rule	16	49
guī	归	歸	to return	19	73
guī	龟	龜	turtle, tortoise	19	73
guō	锅	鍋	wok, pot	20	79
hàn	汗		sweat, perspiration	16	50
hé	盒		box	13	25
hù	互		mutual	15	41
huá	华	華	flowery; Chinese, China	18	71
huán	环	環	ring; to surround	11	7
huáng	皇		emperor; imperial	18	64
jí	及	及	to reach, to come up to	12	17
jí	即		already; completed	14	34
jì	纪	紀	record, annal	13	28
jì	绩	績	achievement, merit	15	43
jì	技		skill	18	68
jì	寄		to mail	19	75
jì	既		already	19	75
jiā	伽		Buddhist temple	14	33
jiǎn	俭	儉	temperate, frugal	17	55
jiàn	渐	漸	gradually	15	39
jiàn	饯	餞	to give a farewell party; preserved food	20	79
jiǎng	讲	講	to speak, to tell	13	27
jiāo	骄	驕	proud, arrogant	15	42
jiē	街		street	12	17
jǐn	尽	儘	to exhaust	12	19
jìng	境		territory	11	7

P	S	T	Definition	L	Page
jiǔ	酒		alcohol, liquor	11	9
jiù	舅		mother's brother, maternal uncle	11	7
jǔ	举	舉	to lift, to raise	11	9
jù	句		(measure word for sentences)	12	19
jù	聚	聚	to gather together	20	79
jù	剧	劇	drama	20	80
jūn	军	軍	army	15	45
kǎn	砍		to cut, to chop	16	50
kè	克		to overcome	16	52
kǒng	孔		opening, hole, a surname	18	70
kǔ	苦	苦	bitter; hardship	17	58
kuà	跨		to cross, to straddle	19	73
kuàng	况	況	circumstance, condition	15	39
kūn	昆		elder brother, descendant	13	29
kuò	括		to include	13	23
lǎn	览	覽	to view	13	26
làng	浪		wave; unrestrained	11	10
lì	利		sharp	11	10
lì	历	曆	calendar	11	11
lì	立		to stand, to establish	18	69
lián	联	聯	to link, to connect	20	81
liàn	炼	煉	to smelt, to refine	14	32
lǐng	领	領	to lead	18	69
lóng	笼	籠	cage	13	28
lū	噜	嚕	rumbling	12	20
ma	嘛	嘛	(particle used to emphasize the obvious)	11	12
mái	霾	霾	haze	16	48
mǎn	满	滿	full; completely	19	73
māo	猫	貓	cat	14	37
máo	矛		spear	17	56
mào	贸	貿	to trade, to barter	18	67
méi	煤		coal	16	49
mèn	闷	悶	depressed	17	57

P	S	T	Definition	L	Page
mián	眠		sleep	14	37
miàn	面	麵	noodles	13	25
miào	庙	廟	temple	12	21
mìng	命		life, fate	18	69
mó	模	模	mold, model	15	41
mò	默		silent	13	25
mù	墓	墓	grave	18	66
nào	闹	鬧	noisy	11	13
Ōu	欧	歐	a surname	20	82
pá	爬		to climb	16	47
pāng	乓		banging sound	15	45
pào	炮		cannon	11	14
péi	赔	賠	to lose (money, etc.), to suffer a loss in a deal	17	60
pīng	乒		sharp, high-pitched sound; ping	15	45
pù	铺	鋪	bunk	13	24
qī	妻		wife	14	31
qí	奇		unusual	11	9
qí	骑	騎	to ride	12	18
qǐ	企		to stand on tiptoe	15	40
qiáng	墙	牆	wall	11	8
Qín	秦		the Qin Dynasty, a surname	18	70
qíng	晴		sunny	19	76
qìng	庆	慶	to celebrate	20	79
qū	区	區	district	11	7
quán	拳		fist, boxing	14	32
quàn	劝	勸	to persuade, to advise, to urge	17	58
quē	缺		to lack	19	76
rǎn	染		to dye	16	51
rēng	扔		to throw, to toss, to throw away	16	48
sàn	散		to scatter	14	32
shā	杀	殺	to kill	18	65
shà	厦	廈	mansion, tall building	12	19
shàn	善	善	good, kind	19	76
shè	摄	攝	to take in, to absorb	16	52

P	S	T	Definition	L	Page
shēng	声	聲	sound	12	20
shèng	剩		to leave a surplus, to be left (over)	11	10
shī	诗	詩	poetry, poem	18	68
shī	湿	濕	wet	19	74
shí	石		stone	13	26
shǐ	使		make	14	34
shì	氏		clan, family	16	52
shì	释	釋	to explain	19	75
shū	输	輸	to lose, to be defeated	15	43
shù	树	樹	tree	13	27
shù	术	術	technique	18	68
shùn	顺	順	smooth	11	9
sī	丝	絲	silk	18	67
Sòng	宋		the Song Dynasty, a surname	18	70
sú	俗		custom	13	26
sù	塑		to mold	16	51
sù	肃	肅	reverent, solemn	19	74
suí	随	隨	to follow	14	34
sūn	孙	孫	grandchild	17	57
tǎ	塔	塔	tower, pagoda	13	27
Táng	唐		the Tang Dynasty, a surname	18	70
tiē	贴	貼	to paste, to glue	11	8
tōng	通		to pass through	13	23
tǒng	统	統	bond	11	11
tǒng	筒		thick tube-shaped object	16	48
tóu	投		to throw, to cast	17	55
tū	突	突	to break through, to protrude; sudden	17	59
tuán	团	團	sphere, lump	11	12
tuì	退		to retreat	14	31
wàn	万	萬	ten thousand	13	28
wěi	伟	偉	big, robust	18	63
wèi	未		not yet	17	57
wēn	温		warm	16	50
wěn	稳	穩	stable	20	80

P	S	T	Definition	L	Page
wò	握		to hold, to grasp	19	77
wū	污	汙	dirty	16	51
wù	雾	霧	fog	16	48
xī	吸	吸	to inhale	14	35
xì	系	繫	to fasten	20	81
xià	吓	嚇	to scare	19	74
xiàn	献	獻	to offer, to present	18	65
xiāng	厢	廂	side room, compartment	13	24
xiǎng	享		to enjoy	13	23
xiāo	宵		night	11	12
xiāo	消		to disappear	15	44
xiāo	销	銷	to sell	19	74
xīn	薪	薪	firewood, salary	15	44
xīn	辛		fiery, laborious	17	58
xióng	熊		bear	14	37
xiū	修	修	to build, to repair	18	65
xū	须	須	must	14	35
yān	烟	菸	smoke, cigarette	14	36
yàn	厌	厭	to dislike	15	42
yáng	阳	陽	sun	16	49
yì	益		benefit	16	47
yì	义	義	righteousness	17	59
yì	谊	誼	friendship	20	81
yīn	阴	陰	overcast, hidden from the sun	19	75
yǐn	引		to draw out, to attract	17	56
yíng	营	營	to manage	14	35
yíng	赢	贏	to win	15	44
yìng	硬		hard	13	24
yǒng	俑		wooden figure buried with the dead	18	67
yǒng	永		always, forever	20	81
yōu	幽		dark, secluded	13	25
yōu	优	優	outstanding, excellent	19	77
yú	余	餘	to have a surplus, to leave some spare	11	10
yú	瑜		flawless gem	14	33
yǔ	与	與	and, with	14	31
yù	郁	鬱	luxuriant, pent-up	17	57
yuán	源		source	16	47
zàn	赞	贊	to praise, to support	16	50
zào	造		to make, to cause	16	52
zēng	增		to increase	17	58
zhǎn	展		to unfold	18	64
zhǎng	涨	漲	to rise, to surge, to go up(of water, prices, etc.)	17	55
zhàng	丈		man, husband	15	41
zhī	之		(literary equivalent of 的)	18	63
zhí	职	職	profession	15	43
zhōu	洲		continent	20	82
zhú	逐		one by one	15	39
zhù	筑	築	to construct	12	18
zhù	注		to concentrate	14	33
zhuàn	赚	賺	to earn, to gain	17	59
zhuāng	装	裝	clothing	12	18
zòng	粽	粽	sticky-rice dumpling wrapped in bamboo or reed leaves	11	11
zuò	座		(measure word for buildings, mountains, bridges, cities and other large, solid things)	12	19

INDEX B

Characters by Lesson and Pinyin

P = pinyin   **S** = simplified form   **T** = traditional form   **L** = lesson

P	S	T	Definition	L	Page
dùn	顿	頓	(measure word for meals)	13	24
gù	故		ancient, former	13	27
guàn	惯	慣	habit	13	26
hé	盒		box	13	25
jì	纪	紀	record, annal	13	28
jiǎng	讲	講	to speak, to tell	13	27
kūn	昆		elder brother, descendant	13	29
kuò	括		to include	13	23
lǎn	览	覽	to view	13	26
lóng	笼	籠	cage	13	28
miàn	面	麵	noodles	13	25
mò	默		silent	13	25
pá	爬		to climb	16	47
pù	铺	鋪	bunk	13	24
shí	石		stone	13	26
shù	树	樹	tree	13	27
sú	俗		custom	13	26
tǎ	塔	塔	tower, pagoda	13	27
tōng	通		to pass through	13	23
wàn	万	萬	ten thousand	13	28
xiāng	厢	廂	side room, compartment	13	24
xiǎng	享		to enjoy	13	23
yìng	硬		hard	13	24
yōu	幽		dark, secluded	13	25
áo	熬	熬	to boil, to stew, to endure	14	36
bǎo	饱	飽	full, satiated (after a meal)	14	35
bì	必		need	14	31
bǔ	补	補	to add, to supplement	14	36
chén	晨		morning	14	33
chōng	充		to fill up	14	36
duàn	锻	鍛	to forge, to temper	14	32
féi	肥		fat	14	34
jí	即		already; completed	14	34
jiā	伽		Buddhist temple	14	33

P	S	T	Definition	L	Page
liàn	炼	煉	to smelt, to refine	14	32
māo	猫	貓	cat	14	37
mián	眠		sleep	14	37
qī	妻		wife	14	31
quán	拳		fist, boxing	14	32
sàn	散		to scatter	14	32
shǐ	使		make	14	34
suí	随	隨	to follow	14	34
tuì	退		to retreat	14	31
xī	吸	吸	to inhale	14	35
xióng	熊		bear	14	37
xū	须	須	must	14	35
yān	烟	菸	smoke, cigarette	14	36
yíng	营	營	to manage	14	35
yú	瑜		flawless gem	14	33
yǔ	与	與	and, with	14	31
zhù	注		to concentrate	14	33
ào	傲		proud, arrogant	15	43
chǎng	厂	廠	factory	15	40
chóu	酬		compensation	15	41
dé	德		virtue, morality	15	45
duì	队	隊	team, a row or line of people, (measure word for teams and lines)	15	42
fàn	范	範	example	15	42
fù	妇	婦	woman	15	39
gǎi	改		to change, to reform	15	40
gé	革		to transform	15	40
guàn	冠		first place	15	44
hù	互		mutual	15	41
jì	绩	績	achievement, merit	15	43
jiàn	渐	漸	gradually	15	39
jiāo	骄	驕	proud, arrogant	15	42
jūn	军	軍	army	15	45
kuàng	况	況	circumstance, condition	15	39
mó	模	模	mold, model	15	41
pāng	乒		banging sound	15	45

P	S	T	Definition	L	Page
gōng	宫	宮	palace	18	65
gòng	贡	貢	to offer tribute	18	64
guān	观	觀	to view	18	63
huá	华	華	flowery; Chinese, China	18	71
huáng	皇		emperor; imperial	18	64
jì	技		skill	18	68
kǒng	孔		opening, hole, a surname	18	70
lì	立		to stand, to establish	18	69
lǐng	领	領	to lead	18	69
mào	贸	貿	to trade, to barter	18	67
mìng	命		life, fate	18	69
mù	墓	墓	grave	18	66
Qín	秦		the Qin Dynasty, a surname	18	70
shā	杀	殺	to kill	18	65
shī	诗	詩	poetry, poem	18	68
shù	术	術	technique	18	68
sī	丝	絲	silk	18	67
Sòng	宋		the Song Dynasty, a surname	18	70
Táng	唐		the Tang Dynasty, a surname	18	70
wěi	伟	偉	big, robust	18	63
xiàn	献	獻	to offer, to present	18	65
xiū	修	修	to build, to repair	18	65
yǒng	俑		wooden figure buried with the dead	18	67
zhǎn	展		to unfold	18	64
zhī	之		(literary equivalent of 的)	18	63
chǎn	产	產	to give birth, to produce	19	76
guī	归	歸	to return	19	73

P	S	T	Definition	L	Page
guī	龟	龜	turtle, tortoise	19	73
jì	寄		to mail	19	75
jì	既		already	19	75
kuà	跨		to cross, to straddle	19	73
mǎn	满	滿	full; completely	19	73
qíng	晴		sunny	19	76
quē	缺		to lack	19	76
shàn	善	善	good, kind	19	76
shī	湿	濕	wet	19	74
shì	释	釋	to explain	19	75
sù	肃	肅	reverent, solemn	19	74
wò	握		to hold, to grasp	19	77
xià	吓	嚇	to scare	19	74
xiāo	销	銷	to sell	19	74
yīn	阴	陰	overcast, hidden from the sun	19	75
yōu	优	優	outstanding, excellent	19	77
chí	池		pool, pound	20	80
gǎo	搞		to do, to carry on, to be engaged in	20	80
guō	锅	鍋	wok, pot	20	79
jiàn	饯	餞	to give a farewell party; preserved food	20	79
jù	聚	聚	to gather together	20	79
jù	剧	劇	drama	20	80
lián	联	聯	to link, to connect	20	81
Ōu	欧	歐	a surname	20	82
qìng	庆	慶	to celebrate	20	79
wěn	稳	穩	stable	20	80
xì	系	繫	to fasten	20	81
yì	谊	誼	friendship	20	81
yǒng	永		always, forever	20	81
zhōu	洲		continent	20	82